FROM THE PUBLISHER

Edith Wharton, having left New York City for Paris in 1906, became an active philanthropist at the outbreak of World War I. Her particular concern was with the plight of Belgian refugees, who fled en masse to Paris after Germany invaded Belgium in 1914. Wharton founded and personally funded the Children of Flanders Relief Committee, but vastly underestimated the length of the war and the expense involved in sustaining refugees for years. *The Book of the Homeless* was conceived as a fundraiser for these refugees, with both a regular edition and 175 deluxe, large format, numbered copies available for purchase.

As both a member of high society in Europe and the United States and an illustrious, globally respected author, Wharton's circle of influence was vast. As described by her, this book was the result of her personally reaching out to her network of friends—authors, artists, musicians, and politicians. The list of contributors is a time capsule of the intellectual and artistic spheres of the early twentieth century. Containing an introduction by President Theodore Roosevelt, new works by authors such as Joseph Conrad and Thomas Hardy, lush watercolors by Monet, and even a score by Stravinsky, *Book of the Homeless* is remarkable—if unclassifiable—in its scope.

THE BOOK OF THE
HOMELESS

(Le Livre des Sans~Foyer)

EDITED BY

EDITH WHARTON

New York & London

MDCCCCXVI

THE BOOK OF THE HOMELESS EDITED BY EDITH WHARTON

(Le Livre des Sans-Foyer)

Original Articles in Verse and Prose
Illustrations reproduced from Original Paintings & Drawings

CALLA EDITIONS
MINEOLA, NEW YORK

The Book of the Homeless, first published by Calla Editions, New York, in 2015, is an unabridged reprint of the edition published by Charles Scriber's Sons, New York, in 1916.

International Standard Book Number

ISBN-13: 978-1-60660-078-8
ISBN-10: 1-60660-078-8

Calla Editions
An Imprint of Dover Publications, Inc.
www.callaeditions.com

Printed in China by C & C Joint Printing CO., (GUANGDONG) LTD

LETTRE DU GÉNÉRAL JOFFRE

Armées de l'Est
Le Commandant en Chef

RÉPUBLIQUE FRANÇAISE

Au Grand Quartier Général, le 18 Août, 1915

Les Etats-Unis d'Amérique n'ont pas oublié que la première page de l'Histoire de leur indépendance a été écrite avec un peu de sang français.

Par leur inépuisable générosité et leur grande sympathie, ils apportent aujourd'hui à la France, qui combat pour sa liberté, l'aide la plus précieuse et le plus puissant réconfort.

J. JOFFRE

LETTER FROM GENERAL JOFFRE

[TRANSLATION]

Headquarters of the Commander-in-chief
of the Armies of the French Republic   *August* 18*th*, 1915

The United States of America have never forgotten that the first page of the history of their independence was partly written in French blood.

Inexhaustibly generous and profoundly sympathetic, these same United States now bring aid and solace to France in the hour of her struggle for liberty.

J. JOFFRE

INTRODUCTION

I⊤ is not only a pleasure but a duty to write the introduction which Mrs. Wharton requests for "The Book of the Homeless." At the outset of this war I said that hideous though the atrocities had been and dreadful though the suffering, yet we must not believe that these atrocities and this suffering paralleled the dreadful condition that had obtained in European warfare during, for example, the seventeenth century. It is lamentable to have to confess that I was probably in error. The fate that has befallen Belgium is as terrible as any that befell the countries of Middle Europe during the Thirty Years' War and the wars of the following half-century. There is no higher duty than to care for the refugees and above all the child refugees who have fled from Belgium. This book is being sold for the benefit of the American Hostels for Refugees and for the benefit of The Children of Flanders Relief Committee, founded in Paris by Mrs. Wharton in November, 1914, and enlarged by her in April, 1915, and chiefly maintained hitherto by American subscriptions. My daughter, who in November and December last was in Paris with her husband, Dr. Derby, in connection with the American Ambulance, has told me much about the harrowing tragedies of the poor souls who were driven from their country and on the verge of starvation, without food or shelter, without hope, and with the members of the family all separated from one another, none knowing where the others were to be found, and who had drifted into Paris and into other parts of France and across the Channel to England as a result of Belgium being trampled into bloody mire. In April last the Belgian Government asked Mrs. Wharton to take charge of some six hundred and fifty children and a number of helpless old men and women from the ruined towns and farms of Flanders. This is the effort which has now turned into The Children of Flanders Rescue Committee.

I appeal to the American people to picture to themselves the plight of these poor creatures and to endeavor in practical fashion to secure that they shall be saved from further avoidable suffering. Nothing that our people can do will remedy the frightful wrong that has been committed on these families. Nothing that can now be done by the civilized world, even if the neutral nations of the civilized world should at last wake up to the performance of the duty they have so shamefully failed to perform, can undo the dreadful wrong of which these unhappy children, these old men and women, have been the victims. All that can be done surely should be done to ease their suffering. The part that America has played in this great tragedy is not an exalted part; and there is all the more reason why Americans should hold up the hands of those of their number who, like Mrs. Wharton, are endeavoring to some extent to remedy the national shortcomings. We owe to Mrs. Wharton all the assistance we can give. We owe this assistance to the good name of America, and above all for the cause of humanity we owe it to the children, the women and the old men who have suffered such dreadful wrong for absolutely no fault of theirs.

THEODORE ROOSEVELT

TABLE OF CONTENTS
CONTRIBUTIONS OF WRITERS AND MUSICIANS

CONTRIBUTIONS OF WRITERS & MUSICIANS

[xiii]

CONTRIBUTIONS OF WRITERS & MUSICIANS

The French poems, except M. Rostand's Sonnet
are translated by Mrs. Wharton

LIST OF ILLUSTRATIONS

CONTRIBUTIONS OF ARTISTS

PREFACE

I

THE HOSTELS

LAST year, among the waifs swept to Paris by the great torrent of the flight from the North, there came to the American Hostels a little acrobat from a strolling circus. He was not much more than a boy, and he had never before been separated from his family or from his circus. All his people were mummers or contortionists, and he himself was a mere mote of the lime-light, knowing life only in terms of the tent and the platform, the big drum, the dancing dogs, the tight-rope and the spangles.

In the sad preoccupied Paris of last winter it was not easy to find a corner for this little figure. But the lad could not be left in the streets, and after a while he was placed as page in a big hotel. He was given good pay, and put into a good livery, and told to be a good boy. He tried . . . he really tried . . . but the life was too lonely. Nobody knew anything about the only things *he* knew, or was particularly interested in the programme of the last performance the company had given at Liège or Maubeuge. The little acrobat could not understand. He told his friends at the Hostels how lonely and puzzled he was, and they tried to help him. But he couldn't sleep at night, because he was used to being up till nearly daylight; and one night he went up to the attic of the hotel, broke open several trunks full of valuables stored there by rich lodgers, and made off with some of the contents. He was caught, of course, and the things he had stolen were produced in court. They were the spangled dresses belonging to a Turkish family, and the embroidered coats of a lady's lap-dog. . . .

I have told this poor little story to illustrate a fact which, as time passes, is beginning to be lost sight of: the fact that we workers among the refugees are trying, first and foremost, to *help a homesick people*. We are not preparing for their new life an army of voluntary colonists; we are seeking to console for the ruin of their old life a throng of bewildered fugitives. It is our business not only to feed and clothe and keep alive these people, but to reassure and guide them. And that has been, for the last year, the task of the American Hostels for Refugees.

The work was started in November, 1914, and since that time we have assisted some 9,300 refugees, given more than 235,000 meals, and distributed 48,333 garments.

But this is only the elementary part of our work. We have done many more difficult things. Our employment agency has found work for over 3,500 men. Our work-rooms occupy about 120 women, and while they sew, their babies are kept busy and happy in a cheerful day-nursery, and the older children are taught in a separate class.

The British Young Women's Christian Association of Paris has shown its interest in our work by supplying us with teachers for the grown-up students who realize the importance of learning English as a part of their business equipment; and these classes are eagerly followed.

Lastly, we have a free clinic where 3,500 sick people have received medical advice, and a dispensary where 4,500 have been given first aid and nursing care; and during the summer we sent many delicate children to the seaside in the care of various Vacation Colonies.

This is but the briefest sketch of our complicated task; a task undertaken a year ago by a small group of French and American friends moved to pity by the thousands of fugitives wandering through the streets of Paris and sleeping on straw in the railway-stations.

We thought then that the burden we were assuming would not have to be borne for more than three or four months, and we were confident of receiving the necessary financial help. We were not mistaken; and America has kept the American Hostels alive for a year. But we are now entering on our second year, with a larger number to care for, and a more delicate task to perform. The longer the exile of these poor people lasts, the more carefully and discriminatingly must we deal with them. They are not all King Alberts and Queen Elisabeths, as some idealists apparently expected them to be. Some are hard to help, others unappreciative of what is done for them. But many, many more are grateful, appreciative, and eager to help us to help them. And of all of them we must say, as Henri de Régnier says for us in the poem written for this Book:

> He who, flying from the fate of slaves
> With brow indignant and with empty hand,
> Has left his house, his country and his graves,
> Comes like a Pilgrim from a Holy Land.
> Receive him thus, if in his blood there be
> One drop of Belgium's immortality.

II

THE CHILDREN

One day last August the members of the "Children of Flanders Rescue Committee" were waiting at the door of the Villa Béthanie, a large seminary near Paris which had been put at the disposal of the committee for the use of the refugee children.

The house stands in a park with fine old trees and a wide view over the lovely rolling country to the northwest of Paris. The day was beautiful, the borders of the drive were glowing with roses, the lawns were fragrant with miniature hay-cocks, and the flower-beds about the court had been edged with garlands of little Belgian flags.

Suddenly we heard a noise of motor-horns, and the gates of the park were thrown open. Down toward us, between the rose-borders, a procession was beginning to pour: first a band of crippled and infirm old men, then a dozen Sisters of Charity in their white caps, and lastly about ninety small boys, each with his little bundle on his back.

They were a lamentable collection of human beings, in pitiful contrast to the summer day and the bright flowers. The old men, for the most part, were too tired and dazed to know where they were, or what was happening to them, and the Sisters were crying from fatigue and home-sickness. The boys looked grave too, but suddenly they caught sight of the flowers, the hay-cocks, and the wide house-front with all its windows smiling in the sun. They took a long look and then, of their own accord, without a hint from their elders, they all broke out together into the Belgian national hymn. The sound of that chorus repaid the friends who were waiting to welcome them for a good deal of worry and hard work.

The flight from western Flanders began last April, when Ypres, Poperinghe, and all the open towns of uninvaded Belgium were swept by a senseless and savage bombardment. Even then it took a long time to induce the inhabitants to give up the ruins of their homes; and before going away themselves they sent their children.

Train-load after train-load of Flemish children poured into Paris last spring. They were gathered in from the ruins, from the trenches, from the hospices where the Sisters of Charity had been caring for them, and where, in many cases, they had been huddled in with the soldiers quartered in the same buildings. Before each convoy started, a young lady with fair hair and very blue eyes walked through the train, distributing chocolate and sandwiches to the children and speaking to each of them in turn, very kindly; and all but the very littlest children understood that this lady was their Queen. . . .

The Belgian government, knowing that I had been working for the refugees, asked me to take charge of sixty little girls, and of the Sisters accompanying them. We found a house, fitted it up, begged for money and clothes, and started The Children of Flanders Rescue Committee. Now, after six months, we have five houses, and are caring for nearly 900 people, among whom are about 200 infirm old men and women whom the Sisters had to bring because there was no one left to look after them in the bombarded towns.

Every war-work, if it has any vitality in it, is bound to increase in this way, and is almost certain to find the help it needs to keep it growing. We have always been so confident of this that we have tried to do for our Children of Flanders what the Hostels have done for the grown-up refugees: not only to feed and clothe and shelter, but also to train and develop them. Some of the Sisters are skilled lace-makers; and we have founded lace-schools in three of our houses. There is a dearth of lace at present, owing to the ruin of the industry in Belgium and Northern France, and our little lace-makers have already received large orders for Valenciennes and other laces. The smallest children are kept busy in classes of the " Montessori" type, provided by the generosity of an American friend, and the boys, out of school-hours, are taught gardening and a little carpentry. We hope later to have the means to enlarge this attempt at industrial training.

This is what we are doing for the Children of Flanders; but, above and beyond all, we are caring for their health and their physical development. The present hope of France and Belgium is in its children, and in the hygienic education of those who have them in charge; and we have taught the good Sisters many things they did not know before concerning the physical care of the children. The results have been better than we could have hoped; and those who saw the arrival of the piteous waifs a few months ago would scarcely recognize them in the round and rosy children playing in the gardens of our Houses.

III

THE BOOK

I said just now that when we founded our two refugee charities we were confident of getting money enough to carry them on. So we were; and so we had a right to be; for at the end of the first twelvemonth we are still alive and solvent.

But we never dreamed, at the start, that the work would last longer than a year, or that its demands would be so complex and increasing. And when we saw before us the certainty of having to carry this poor burden of humanity for another twelve months, we began to wonder how we should get the help to do it.

Then the thought of this Book occurred to me. I appealed to my friends who write and paint and compose, and they to other friends of theirs, writers, painters, composers, statesmen and dramatic artists; and so the Book gradually built itself up, page by page and picture by picture.

You will see from the names of the builders what a gallant piece of architecture it is, what delightful pictures hang on its walls, and what noble music echoes through them. But what I should have liked to show is the readiness, the kindliness, the eagerness, with which all the collaborators, from first to last, have lent a hand to the building. Perhaps you will guess it for yourselves when you read their names and see the beauty and variety of what they have given. So I efface myself from the threshold and ask you to walk in.

EDITH WHARTON

Paris, November, 1915

Gifts of money for the American Hostels for Refugees, and the Children of Flanders Rescue Committee should be addressed to Mrs. Wharton, 53 rue de Varenne, Paris, or to Henry W. Munroe, Treasurer, care of Mrs. Cadwalader Jones, 21 East Eleventh Street, New York.

Gifts in kind should be forwarded to the American War Relief Clearing House, 5 rue François Ier, Paris (*with Mrs. Wharton's name in the left-hand corner*), *via* the American offices of the Clearing House, 15 Broad Street, New York.

I

POETRY

CONTRIBUTORS OF POETRY AND MUSIC

LAURENCE BINYON

RUPERT BROOKE

PAUL CLAUDEL

JEAN COCTEAU

ROBERT GRANT

THOMAS HARDY

W. D. HOWELLS

FRANCIS JAMMES

ALICE MEYNELL

COMTESSE DE NOAILLES

JOSEPHINE PRESTON PEABODY

LILLA CABOT PERRY

HENRI DE RÉGNIER

EDMOND ROSTAND

GEORGE SANTAYANA

EDITH M. THOMAS

HERBERT TRENCH

ÉMILE VERHAEREN

BARRETT WENDELL

EDITH WHARTON

MARGARET L. WOODS

W. B. YEATS

∴

IGOR STRAVINSKY

VINCENT D'INDY

THE ORPHANS OF FLANDERS

WHERE is the land that fathered, nourished, poured
The sap of a strong race into your veins,—
Land of wide tilth, of farms and granaries stored,
And old towers chiming over peaceful plains?

It is become a vision, barred away
Like light in cloud, a memory, a belief.
On those lost plains the Glory of yesterday
Builds her dark towers for the bells of Grief.

It is become a splendour-circled name
For all the world. A torch against the skies
Burns from that blood-spot, the unpardoned shame
Of them that conquered: but your homeless eyes

See rather some brown pond by a white wall,
Red cattle crowding in the rutty lane,
Some garden where the hollyhocks were tall
In the Augusts that shall never be again.

There your thoughts cling as the long-thrusting root
Clings in the ground; your orphaned hearts are there.
O mates of sunburnt earth, your love is mute
But strong like thirst and deeper than despair.

You have endured what pity can but grope
To feel; into that darkness enters none.
We have but hands to help: yours is the hope
Whose silent courage rises with the sun.

LAURENCE BINYON

[3]

THE DANCE

A SONG

As the Wind and as the Wind
      In a corner of the way,
Goes stepping, stands twirling,
Invisibly, comes whirling,
Bows before and skips behind
      In a grave, an endless play—

So my Heart and so my Heart
      Following where your feet have gone,
Stirs dust of old dreams there;
He turns a toe; he gleams there,
Treading you a dance apart.
      But you see not. You pass on.

RUPERT BROOKE

THÉO VAN RYSSELBERGHE

PORTRAIT OF ANDRÉ GIDE

FROM A PENCIL DRAWING

LE PRÉCIEUX SANG

—Seigneur, qui pour un verre d'eau nous avez promis
la mer illimitée,
  Qui sait si vous n'avez pas soif aussi?
Et que ce sang qui est tout ce que nous avons soit propre
à vous désaltérer,
  C'est vrai, puisque vous l'avez dit!
Si vraiment il y a une source en nous, eh bien, c'est ce
que nous allons voir!
  Si ce vin a quelque vertu
Et si notre sang est rouge, comme vous le dites, com-
ment le savoir
  Autrement que quand il est répandu?
Si notre sang est vraiment précieux, comme vous le dites,
si vraiment il est comme de l'or,
  S'il sert, pourquoi le garder?
Et sans savoir ce qu'on peut acheter avec, pourquoi le
réserver comme un trésor,
  Mon Dieu, quand vous nous le demandez?
Nos péchés sont grands, nous le savons, et qu'il faut
absolument faire pénitence,
  Mais il est difficile pour un homme de pleurer.
Voici notre sang au lieu de larmes que nous avons ré-
pandu pour la France:
  Faites-en ce que vous voudrez.
Prenez-le, nous vous le donnons, tirez-en vous-même
usage et bénéfice,
  Nous ne vous faisons point de demande

Mais si vous avez besoin de notre amour autant que nous
avons besoin de votre justice,
Alors c'est que votre soif est grande!

P. CLAUDEL

Juillet 1915

THE PRECIOUS BLOOD

[TRANSLATION]

OH, what if Thou, that for a cup of water promisest
The illimitable sea,
Thou, Lord, dost also thirst?
Hast Thou not said, our blood shall quench Thee best
And first
    Of any drink there be?

If then there be such virtue in it, Lord,
Ah, let us prove it now!
And, save by seeing it at Thy footstool poured,
    How, Lord—oh, how?

If it indeed be precious and like gold,
As Thou hast taught,
Why hoard it? There's no wealth in gems unsold,
    Nor joy in gems unbought.

Our sins are great, we know it; and we know
We must redeem our guilt;
Even so.

[6]

PAUL CLAUDEL

But tears are difficult for a man to shed,
And here is our blood poured out for France instead,
    To do with as Thou wilt!

Take it, O Lord! And make it Thine indeed,
Void of all lien and fee.
Nought else we ask of Thee;
But if Thou needst our Love as we Thy Justice need,
    Great must Thine hunger be!

PAUL CLAUDEL

LÉON BAKST

PORTRAIT OF JEAN COCTEAU

JEAN COCTEAU

LA MORT DES JEUNES GENS DE LA DIVINE HELLADE

FRAGMENT

ANTIGONE criant et marchant au supplice
N'avait pas de la mort leur sublime respect;
Ce n'était pas pour eux une funeste paix,
C'était un ordre auquel il faut qu'on obéisse.

Ils ne subissaient pas l'offense qu'il fît beau
Que le soleil mûrît les grappes de glycine;
Ils étaient souriant en face du tombeau,
Les rossignols élus que la rose assassine.

Ils ne regrettaient pas les tendres soirs futurs,
Les conversations sur les places d'Athènes,
Où, le col altéré de poussière et d'azur,
Pallas, comme un pigeon, pleure au bord des fontaines.

Ils ne regrettaient pas les gradins découverts
Où le public trépigne, insiste,
Pour regarder, avant qu'ils montent sur la piste,
Les cochers bleus riant avec les cochers verts.

Ils ne regrettaient pas ce loisir disparate
D'une ville qui semble un sordide palais,
Où l'on se réunit pour entendre Socrate
Et pour jouer aux osselets.

Ils étaient éblouis de tumulte et de risque,
Mais, si la fourbe mort les désignait soudain,

Ils laissaient sans gémir sur l'herbe du jardin
Les livres et le disque.

Ce n'était pas pour eux l'insupportable affront,
Ils se couchaient sans choc, sans lutte, sans tapage,
Comme on voit, ayant bien remué sous le front,
Un vers définitif s'étendre sur la page.

Ils étaient résignés, vêtus, rigides, prêts
Pour cette expérience étrange,
Comme Hyacinthe en fleur indolemment se change
Et comme Cyparis se transforme en cyprès.

Ils ne regrettaient rien de vivre en Ionie,
D'être libres, d'avoir des mères et des sœurs,
Et de sentir ce lourd sommeil envahisseur
Après une courte insomnie.

Ils rentraient au séjour qui n'a plus de saison,
Où notre faible orgueil se refuse à descendre,
Sachant que l'urne étroite où gît un peu de cendre
Sera tout le jardin et toute la maison.

Jadis j'ai vu mourir des frères de mon âge,
J'ai vu monter en eux l'indicible torpeur.
Ils avaient tous si mal! Ils avaient tous si peur!
Ils se prenaient la tête avec des mains en nage.

Ils ne pouvaient pas croire, ayant si soif, si faim,
Un tel désir de tout avec un cœur si jeune,
A ce désert sans source, à cet immense jeûne,
A ce terme confus qui n'a jamais de fin.

Ils n'attendaient plus rien de la tendresse humaine
Et cherchaient à chasser d'un effort douloureux
L'Ange noir qui se couche à plat ventre sur eux
Et qui les considère avant qu'il les emmène.

JEAN COCTEAU

HOW THE YOUNG MEN DIED IN HELLAS

A FRAGMENT

[TRANSLATION]

ANTIGONE went wailing to the dust.
She reverenced not the face of Death like these
To whom it came as no enfeebling peace
But a command relentless and august.

These grieved not at the beauty of the morn,
Nor that the sun was on the ripening flower;
Smiling they faced the sacrificial hour,
Blithe nightingales against the fatal thorn.

They grieved not that their feet no more should rove
The Athenian porticoes in twilight leisure,
Where Pallas, drunk with summer's gold and azure,
Brooded above the fountains like a dove.

They grieved not for the theatre's high-banked tiers,
Where restlessly the noisy crowd leans over,
With laughter and with jostling, to discover
The blue and green of chaffing charioteers.

Nor for the fluted shafts, the carven stones
Of that sole city, bright above the seas,
Where young men met to talk with Socrates
      Or toss the ivory bones.

Their eyes were lit with tumult and with risk,
But when they felt Death touch their hands and pass
They followed, dropping on the garden grass
      The parchment and the disk.

It seemed no wrong to them that they must go.
They laid their lives down as the poet lays
On the white page the poem that shall praise
His memory when the hand that wrote is low.

Erect they stood and, festally arrayed,
Serenely waited the transforming hour,
Softly as Hyacinth slid from youth to flower,
Or the shade of Cyparis to a cypress shade.

They wept not for the lost Ionian days,
Nor liberty, nor household love and laughter,
Nor the long leaden slumber that comes after
      Life's little wakefulness.

Fearless they sought the land no sunsets see,
Whence our weak pride shrinks back, and would return,
Knowing a pinch of ashes in an urn
Henceforth our garden and our house shall be.

Young men, my brothers, you whose morning skies
I have seen the deathly lassitude invade,

JEAN COCTEAU

Oh, how you suffered! How you were afraid!
What death-damp hands you locked about your eyes!

You, so insatiably athirst to spend
The young desires in your hearts abloom,
How could you think the desert was your doom,
The waterless fountain and the endless end?

You yearned not for the face of love, grown dim,
But only fought your anguished bones to wrest
From the Black Angel crouched upon your breast,
Who scanned you ere he led you down with him.

JEAN COCTEAU

A MESSAGE

This is our gift to the Homeless.
  What shall it bear from me
Safe in a land that prospers
  Girded by leagues of sea?—
Tear moistened words of pity,
  Bountiful sympathy.

Clearly we see the picture,
  Horror has fixed our eyes.
Fighting to guard its hearthstones
  A nation mangled lies.
Fire has charred its beauty,
  Murder has stilled its cries;

And truths we love and cherish
  Hang in the trembling scale.
If you win, we win by proxy,
  If you fail, we are doomed to fail.
The world is beset by a monster,
  Yet we watch to see who shall prevail.

Our souls are racked and quickened,
  But prudence counsels no.
So we lavish our gold and pity
  And wait to see how it will go,—
This pivotal war of the ages
  With its heartrending ebb and flow.

ROBERT GRANT

For ever there comes the moment
   When destiny bids "choose."
By the edge of the sword men perish,
   By selfishness all they lose.
So Belgium stands transfigured
   As the one who did not refuse.

ROBERT GRANT

CRY OF THE HOMELESS

INSTIGATOR of the ruin—
　　Whichsoever thou mayst be
Of the mastering minds of Europe
　　That contrived our misery—
Hear the wormwood-worded greeting
　　From each city, shore, and lea
　　　　Of thy victims:
"Enemy, all hail to thee!"

Yea: "All hail!" we grimly shout thee
　　That wast author, fount, and head
Of these wounds, whoever proven
　　When our times are throughly read.
"May thy dearest ones be blighted
　　And forsaken," be it said
　　　　By thy victims,
"And thy children beg their bread!"

Nay: too much the malediction.—
　　Rather let this thing befall
In the unfurling of the future,
　　On the night when comes thy call:
That compassion dew thy pillow
　　And absorb thy senses all
　　　　For thy victims,
Till death dark thee with his pall.

　　　　　　　　THOMAS HARDY

August, 1915

JACQUES-ÉMILE BLANCHE

PORTRAIT OF THOMAS HARDY

FROM A PHOTOGRAPH OF THE ORIGINAL PAINTING

To Mr Thomas Hardy; J. E. Blanche
28 May 1906
London

THE LITTLE CHILDREN

"Suffer little children to come unto me,"
  Christ said, and answering with infernal glee,
"Take them!" the arch-fiend scoffed, and from the tottering walls
  Of their wrecked homes, and from the cattle's stalls,
  And the dogs' kennels, and the cold
  Of the waste fields, and from the hapless hold
  Of their dead mothers' arms, famished and bare,
  And maimed by shot and shell,
  The master-spirit of hell
  Caught them up, and through the shuddering air
  Of the hope-forsaken world
  The little ones he hurled,
  Mocking that Pity in his pitiless might—
  The Anti-Christ of Schrecklickeit.

W. D. Howells

ÉPITAPHE

Cɪ-ɢɪт un tel, mort pour la France et qui, vivant,
Poussait sa voiturette à travers les villages
Pour vendre un peu de fil, de sel ou de fromage,
Sous les portails d'azur aux feuillages mouvants.

Il a gagné son pain comme au Commandement
Que donne aux hommes Dieu dans le beau Livre sage.
Puis, un jour, sur sa tête a crevé le nuage
Que lance l'orageux canon de l'Allemand.

Ce héros, dans l'éclair qui délivra son âme,
Aura vu tout en noir ses enfants et sa femme
Contemplants anxieux son pauvre gagne-pain:

Ce chariot plus beau que n'est celui de l'Ourse
Et qu'il a fait rouler pendant la dure course
Qui sur terre commence un céleste destin.

Fʀᴀɴᴄɪs Jᴀᴍᴍᴇs

Orthez, 29 *Juillet* 1915

FRANCIS JAMMES

AN EPITAPH

[TRANSLATION]

HERE such an one lies dead for France. His trade
To push a barrow stocked with thread, cheese, salt
From town to town, under the azure vault,
Through endless corridors of rustling shade.
True to the sacred law of toil, he made
His humble living as the Book commands,
Till suddenly there burst upon his lands
The thunder of the German cannonade.

Poor hero! In the flash that smote him dead
He saw his wife and children all in black
Weeping about the cart that earned their bread—
The cart that, by his passionate impulse sped
On immortality's celestial track,
Shone brighter than the Wain above his head.

FRANCIS JAMMES

IN SLEEP

I DREAMT (no "dream" awake—a dream indeed)
A wrathful man was talking in the Park:
"Where are the Higher Powers who know our need,
    Yet leave us in the dark?

"There are no Higher Powers; there is no heart
In God, no love"—his oratory here,
Taking the paupers' and the cripples' part,
    Was broken by a tear.

And next it seemed that One who did invent
Compassion, who alone created pity,
Walked, as though called, and hastened as He went
    Out from the muttering city;

Threaded the little crowd, trod the brown grass,
Bent o'er the speaker close, saw the tear rise,
And saw Himself, as one looks in a glass,
    In those impassioned eyes.

ALICE MEYNELL

COMTESSE DE NOAILLES

NOS MORTS

Astres qui regardez les mondes où nous sommes,
Pure armée au repos dans la hauteur des cieux,
Campement éternel, léger, silencieux,
Que pensez-vous de voir s'anéantir les hommes?
A n'être pas sublime aucun ne condescend,
Comme un cri vers la nue on voit jaillir leur sang
Qui sur nos cœurs contrits lentement se rabaisse.
—Morts divins, portez-nous un plausible secours!
Notre douleur n'est pas la sœur de votre ivresse.
Vous mourez! Concevez que c'est un poids trop lourd
Pour ceux qui dans leur grave et brûlante tristesse
Ont toujours confondu la Vie avec l'Amour.

Comtesse de Noailles

OUR DEAD

[TRANSLATION]

Stars that behold our world upon its way,
Pure legions camped upon the plains of night,
Mute watchful hosts of heaven, what must you say
When men destroy each other in their might?
Upon their deadly race each runner starts,
Nor one but will his brothers all outrun!
Ah, see their blood jet upward to the sun
Like living fountains refluent on our hearts!
O dead divinely for so great a faith,

Help us, whose agony is but begun,
For bitterly we yield you up to death,
We who had dreamed that Life and Love were one.

COMTESSE DE NOAILLES

CLAUDE MONET

LANDSCAPE

TWO SONGS OF A YEAR

1914–1915

I

CHILDREN'S KISSES

So; it is nightfall then.
The valley flush
That beckoned home the way for herds and men
Is hardly spent:
Down the bright pathway winds, through veils of hush
And wonderment.
Unuttered yet the chime
That tells of folding-time;
Hardly the sun has set;—
The trees are sweetly troubled with bright words
From new-alighted birds.
And yet, . . .
Here, round my neck, are come to cling and twine,
The arms, the folding arms, close, close and fain,
All mine!—
I pleaded to, in vain,
I reached for, only to their dimpled scorning,
Down the blue halls of morning;—
Where all things else could lure them on and on,
Now here, now gone,
From bush to bush, from beckoning bough to bough,
With bird-calls of *Come Hither!*—

Ah, but now . . .
Now it is dusk.—And from his heaven of mirth,

A wilding skylark sudden dropt to earth
Along the last low sunbeam yellow-moted,—
Athrob with joy,—
There pushes here, a little golden Boy,
Still gazing with great eyes:
And wonder-wise,
All fragrancy, all valor silver-throated,
My daughterling, my swan,
My Alison.

Closer than homing lambs against the bars
At folding-time, that crowd, all mother-warm,
They crowd, they cling, they wreathe;—
And thick as sparkles of the thronging stars,
Their kisses swarm.

O Rose of Being at whose heart I breathe,
Fold over, hold me fast
In the dim Eden of a blinding kiss.
And lightning heart's desire, be still at last.
Heart can no more,—
Life can no more
Than this.

II

THE SANS-FOYER

Love, that Love cannot share,—
　　　Now turn to air!
And fade to ashes, O my daily bread,
　　　Save only if you may
　　　Bless you, to be the stay
　　　Of the uncomforted.

Behold, you far-off lights,—
　　　From smoke-veiled heights,
If there be dwelling in our wilderness!
　　　For Love the refugee,
　　　No stronghold can there be,—
No shelter more, while these go shelterless.

Love hath no home, beside
　　　His own two arms spread wide;—
The only home, among all walls that are:
　　　So there may come to cling,
　　　Some yet forlorner thing
Feeling its way, along this blackened star.

　　　　　JOSEPHINE PRESTON PEABODY

RAIN IN BELGIUM

THE heavy rain falls down, falls down,
On city streets whence all have fled,
Where tottering ruins skyward frown
Above the staring silent dead.
Here shall ye raise your Kaiser's throne,
Stained with the blood for freedom shed.

Here where men choked for breath in vain
Who in fair fight had all withstood,
Here on this poison-haunted plain,
Made rich with babes' and women's blood,
Here shall ye plant your German grain,
Here shall ye reap your children's food.

The harvest ripens—Reaper come!
Bring children singing Songs of Hate
Taught by the mother in the home—
Fit comrade she for such a mate.
Soon shall ye reap what ye have sown;
God's mills grind thoroughly though late.

The heavy rain beats down, beats down;
I hear in it the tramp of Fate!

LILLA CABOT PERRY

L'EXILÉ

"O DEUIL de ne pouvoir emporter sur la mer
Dans l'écume salée et dans le vent amer,
L'épi de son labeur et le fruit de sa treille,
Ni la rose que l'aurore fait plus vermeille
Ni rien de tout de ce qui, selon chaque saison,
Pare divinement le seuil de la maison!
Mais, puisque mon foyer n'est plus qu'un peu de cendre,
Et que, dans mon jardin, je ne dois plus entendre
Sur les arbres chanter les oiseaux du printemps;
Que nul ne reviendra de tous ceux que j'attends,
S'abriter sous le toit où nichaient les colombes,
Adieu donc, doux pays où nous avions nos tombes,
Où nous devions, à l'heure où se ferment les yeux,
Nous endormir auprès du sommeil des aïeux!
Nous partons. Ne nous pleurez pas, tendres fontaines,
Terre que nous quittons pour des terres lointaines,
O toi que le brutal talon du conquérant
A foulée et qu'au loin, de sa lueur de sang,
Empourpre la bataille et rougit l'incendie!
Qu'un barbare vainqueur nous chasse et qu'il châtie
En nous le saint amour que nous avons pour toi,
C'est bien. La force pour un jour, prime le droit,
Mais l'exil qu'on subit pour ta cause, Justice,
Laisse au destin vengeur le temps qu'il s'accomplisse.
Nous reviendrons. Et soit que nous passions la mer
Parmi l'embrun cinglant et dans le vent amer,
Soit que le sort cruel rudement nous disperse,
Troupeau errant, sous la rafale ou sous l'averse,

Ne nous plains pas, cher hôte, en nous tendant la main,
Car n'est-il pas pour toi un étranger divin
Celui qui, le front haut et les yeux pleins de flamme,
A quitté sa maison pour fuir un joug infâme
Et dont le fier genou n'a pas voulu ployer
Et qui, pauvre, exilé, sans pain et sans foyer,
Sent monter, de son cœur à sa face pâlie,
Ce même sang sacré que saigne la Patrie.

HENRI DE RÉGNIER
de l'Académie Française

THE EXILE

[TRANSLATION]

BITTER our fate, that may not bear away
On the harsh winds and through the alien spray
Sheaves of our fields and fruit from the warm wall,
The rose that reddens at the morning's call,
Nor aught of all wherewith the turning year
Our doorway garlanded, from green to sere. . . .
But since the ash is cold upon the hearth,
And dumb the birds in garden and in garth,
Since none shall come again, of all our loves,
Back to this roof that crooned with nesting doves,
Now let us bid farewell to all our dead,
And that dear corner of earth where they are laid,
And where in turn it had been good to lay
Our kindred heads on the appointed day.

Weep not, O springs and fountains, that we go,
And thou, dear earth, the earth our footsteps know,

HENRI DE RÉGNIER

Weep not, thou desecrated, shamed and rent,
Consumed with fire and with blood-shed spent.
Small strength have they that hunt us from thy fold
To loosen love's indissoluble hold,
And brighter than the flames about thy pyre
Our exiled faith shall spring for thee, and higher.
We shall return. Let Time reverse the glass.
Homeless and scattered from thy face we pass,
Through rain and tempest flying from our doors,
On seas unfriendly swept to stranger shores.
But, O you friends unknown that wait us there,
We ask no pity, though your bread we share.
For he who, flying from the fate of slaves
With brow indignant and with empty hand,
Has left his house, his country and his graves,
Comes like a Pilgrim from a Holy Land.
Receive him thus, if in his blood there be
One drop of Belgium's immortality.

HENRI DE RÉGNIER
de l'Académie Française

HORREUR ET BEAUTÉ

Sabreur de mains d'enfants qui demandaient du pain,
Brûleur de basilique et de bibliothèque,
Geste obscène, œil sanglant, front d'anthropopithèque,
L'homme ne s'est jamais plus hideusement peint.

Mais Roncevaux n'a rien de plus beau, sous son Pin,
Rien de plus pur, sous son Laurier, la fable Grecque,
Que ce jeune Monarque et son vieil Archevêque:
C'est Achille et Nestor, c'est Roland et Turpin.

Roi, d'un juste reflux puissions-nous voir la vague!
Et toi, puisque ta main éleva dans sa bague
Le seul reflet de ciel qui bénit cet Enfer,

Que la pourpre sur toi soit plus cardinalice,
Prêtre! et que de la Croix qui n'était pas de Fer
Un Christ plus abondant coule dans ton calice!

EDMOND ROSTAND

EDMOND ROSTAND

HORROR AND BEAUTY

[TRANSLATION]

GASHED hands of children who cry out for bread—
　　While as the flames from sacred places rise
The Blonde Beast, hideous, with blood-shot eyes
　　And obscene gesture mutilates the dead—

But neither Roncesvalles where Roland bled
　　With Turpin, nor Greek deeds of high emprise
Can to a pitch of purer beauty rise
　　Than the Young King, the Priest, unconqueréd.

Oh King, soon all thy foes may'st thou repel!
　　And thou, High-Priest, from whose ring, raised to men,
Shone the one gleam of Heaven in that Hell,

May thy empurpled vestments so avail
　　That from the Cross—not made of Iron then—
A richer Christ glow in thy holy grail.

EDMOND ROSTAND

Translated by Walter V. R. Berry

THE UNDERGRADUATE KILLED IN BATTLE

Sᴡᴇᴇᴛ as the lawn beneath his sandalled tread
Or the scarce rippled stream beneath his oar,
For its still, channelled current constant more,
His life was, and the few blithe words he said.

One or two poets read he, and reread;
One or two friends in boyish ardour wore
Next to his heart, incurious of the lore
Dodonian woods might murmur o'er his head.

Ah, demons of the whirlwind, have a care
What, trumpeting your triumphs, ye undo!
The earth once won, begins your long despair
That never, never is his bliss for you.
He breathed betimes this clement island air
And in unwitting lordship saw the blue.

GᴇᴏʀɢᴇSᴀɴᴛᴀʏᴀɴᴀ

Oxford, August, 1915

WALTER GAY

INTERIOR

FROM AN ORIGINAL WATER-COLOUR SKETCH

EDITH M. THOMAS

THE CHILDREN AND THE FLAG

The little children in my country kiss the American flag.
MADAME VANDERVELDE

WHAT of those children over the sea
That are beating about the world's rough ways,
Like the tender blossoms from off a tree
That a sudden gale in Spring betrays?
The children? Oh, let them look for the sign
Of a wave-borne flag, thou land of mine!

On the old gray sea its course it holds,
Life for the famished is in its gift. . . .
And the children are crowding to kiss its folds,
While the tears of their mothers fall free and swift.—
And what of the flag their lips have pressed?
Oh, guard it for ever—That flag is blest.

EDITH M. THOMAS

THE TROUBLER OF TELARO

1

WARM vines bloom now along thy rampart steeps
Thy shelves of olives, undercliffs of azure,
And like a lizard of the red rock sleeps
The wrinkled Tuscan sea, panting for pleasure.
Nets, too, festooned about thine elfin port,
Telaro, in the Etrurian mountain's side,
Heavings of golden luggers scarce distort
The image of thy belfry where they ride.
But thee, Telaro, on a night long gone
That grey and holy tower upon the mole
Suddenly summoned, while yet lightnings shone
And hard gale lingered, with a ceaseless toll
That choked, with its disastrous monotone,
All the narrow channels of the hamlet's soul.

2

For what despair, fire, shipwreck, treachery?
Was it for threat that from the macchia sprang
For Genoa's feud, the oppressor's piracy,
Or the Falcon of Sarzana that it rang?
Was the boat-guild's silver plundered? Blood should pay.
Hardwon the footing of the fishers' clan
The sea-cloud-watchers.—Loud above the spray
The maddening iron cry, the appeal of man,
Washed through the torchless midnight on and on.
Are not enough the jeopardies of day?
Riot arose—fear's Self began the fray:

But the tower proved empty. By the lightning's ray
They found no human ringer in the room. . . .
The bell-rope quivered out in the sea-spume. . . .

3

A creature fierce, soft, witless of itself,
A morbid mouth, circled by writhing arms,
By its own grasp entangled on that shelf,
Had dragged the rope and spread the death-alarms;
Insensitive, light-forgotten, up from slime,
From shelter betwixt rocks, issuing for prey
Disguised, had used man's language of dismay.
The spawn of perished times had late in time
Emerged, and griefs upon man's grief imposed
Incalculable.

But the fishers closed
The blind mouth, and cut off the suckers cold.
Two thousand fathoms the disturber rolled
From trough to trough into the gulf Tyrrhene;
And fear sank with it back into its night obscene.

HERBERT TRENCH

THÉO VAN RYSSELBERGHE

PORTRAIT OF ÉMILE VERHAEREN

FROM A PENCIL DRAWING

Août 1915

ÉMILE VERHAEREN

LE PRINTEMPS DE 1915

Tu me disais de ta voix douce,
Tu me disais en insistant:
—Y a-t-il encor un Printemps
Et les feuilles repoussent-elles?

La guerre accapare le ciel
Les eaux, les monts, les bois, la terre:
Où sont les fleurs couleur de miel
Pour les abeilles volontaires?

Où sont les pousses des roncerois
Et les boutons des anémones?
Où sont les flûtes dans les bois
Des oiseaux sombres aux becs jaunes?

—Hélas! plus n'est de floraison
Que celle des feux dans l'espace:
Bouquet de rage et de menace
S'éparpillant sur l'horizon.

Plus n'est, hélas! de splendeur rouge
Que celle, hélas! des boulets fous
Éclaboussant de larges coups
Clochers, hameaux, fermes et bouges.

C'est le printemps de ce temps-ci:
Le vent répand de plaine en plaine,

Là-bas, ces feuillaisons de haine;
C'est la terreur de ce temps-ci.

ÉMILE VERHAEREN

Saint-Cloud, le 31 *Juillet* 1915

THE NEW SPRING

[TRANSLATION]

SADLY your dear voice said:
"Is the old spring-time dead,
And shall we never see
New leaves upon the tree?

"Shall the black wings of war
Blot out sun, moon and star,
And never a bud unfold
To the bee its secret gold?

"Where are the wind-flowers streaked,
And the wayward bramble shoots,
And the black-birds yellow-beaked
With a note like woodland flutes?"

No flower shall bloom this year
But the wild flame of fear
Wreathing the evil night
With burst of deadly light.

ÉMILE VERHAEREN

No splendour of petals red
But that which the cannon shed,
Raining their death-bloom down
On farm and tower and town.

This is the scarlet doom
By the wild sea-winds hurled
Over a land of gloom,
Over a grave-strewn world.

ÉMILE VERHAEREN

1915

Though desolation stain their foiled advance,
  In ashen ruins hearth-stones linger whole:
Do what they may, they cannot master France;
  Do what they can, they cannot quell the soul.

Barrett Wendell

THE TRYST

I SAID to the woman: Whence do you come,
With your bundle in your hand?
She said: In the North I made my home,
Where slow streams fatten the fruitful loam,
And the endless wheat-fields run like foam
To the edge of the endless sand.

I said: What look have your houses there,
And the rivers that glass your sky?
Do the steeples that call your people to prayer
Lift fretted fronts to the silver air,
And the stones of your streets, are they washed and fair
When the Sunday folk go by?

My house is ill to find, she said,
For it has no roof but the sky;
The tongue is torn from the steeple-head,
The streets are foul with the slime of the dead,
And all the rivers run poison-red
With the bodies drifting by.

I said: Is there none to come at your call
In all this throng astray?
They shot my husband against a wall,
And my child (she said), too little to crawl,
Held up its hands to catch the ball
When the gun-muzzle turned its way.

I said: There are countries far from here
Where the friendly church-bells call,
And fields where the rivers run cool and clear,
And streets where the weary may walk without fear,
And a quiet bed, with a green tree near,
To sleep at the end of it all.

She answered: Your land is too remote,
And what if I chanced to roam
When the bells fly back to the steeples' throat,
And the sky with banners is all afloat,
And the streets of my city rock like a boat
With the tramp of her men come home?

I shall crouch by the door till the bolt is down,
And then go in to my dead.
Where my husband fell I will put a stone,
And mother a child instead of my own,
And stand and laugh on my bare hearth-stone
When the King rides by, she said.

EDITH WHARTON

Paris, August 27th, 1915

P. A. J. DAGNAN-BOUVERET

BRITTANY WOMAN

FROM A DRAWING IN COLOURED CRAYONS

FINISTERRE

O THAT on some forsaken strand,
Lone ending of a lonely land,
On such an eve we two were lying,
To hear the quiet water sighing
And feel the coolness of the sand.

A red and broken moon would grow
Out of the dusk and even so
As here to-night the street she faces,
Between the half-distinguished spaces
Of sea and sky would burn and go.

The moon would go and overhead,
Like tapers lighted o'er the dead,
Star after silver star would glimmer,
The lonely night grow calmer, dimmer,
The quiet sea sink in its bed.

We, at the end of Time and Fate,
Might unconcerned with love or hate
As the sea's voices, talk together,
Wherefore we went apart and whither,
And all the exiled years relate.

Thus were life's grey chance-'ravelled sleave'
Outspread, we something might perceive
Which never would to chance surrender,
But through the tangled woof its slender
Golden, elusive pattern weave.

Then while the great stars larger shone
Leaned on the sea, and drew thereon
Faint paths of light, across them faring
Might steal the ship that comes for bearing
Sore-wounded souls to Avalon.

MARGARET L. WOODS

A REASON FOR KEEPING SILENT

I THINK it better that at times like these
We poets keep our mouths shut, for in truth
We have no gift to set a statesman right;
He's had enough of meddling who can please
A young girl in the indolence of her youth
Or an old man upon a winter's night.

W. B. YEATS

JACQUES-ÉMILE BLANCHE

PORTRAIT OF IGOR STRAVINSKY

FROM A STUDY IN OILS

MUSICAL SCORE

IGOR STRAVINSKY

SOUVENIR D'UNE MARCHE BOCHE

THÉO VAN RYSSELBERGHE

PORTRAIT OF VINCENT D'INDY

FROM A PHOTOGRAPH OF THE ORIGINAL PAINTING

MUSICAL SCORE

VINCENT D'INDY

LA LÉGENDE DE SAINT CHRISTOPHE

PAGE OF SCORE OF UNPUBLISHED OPERA

[ACTE I, SCÈNE III]

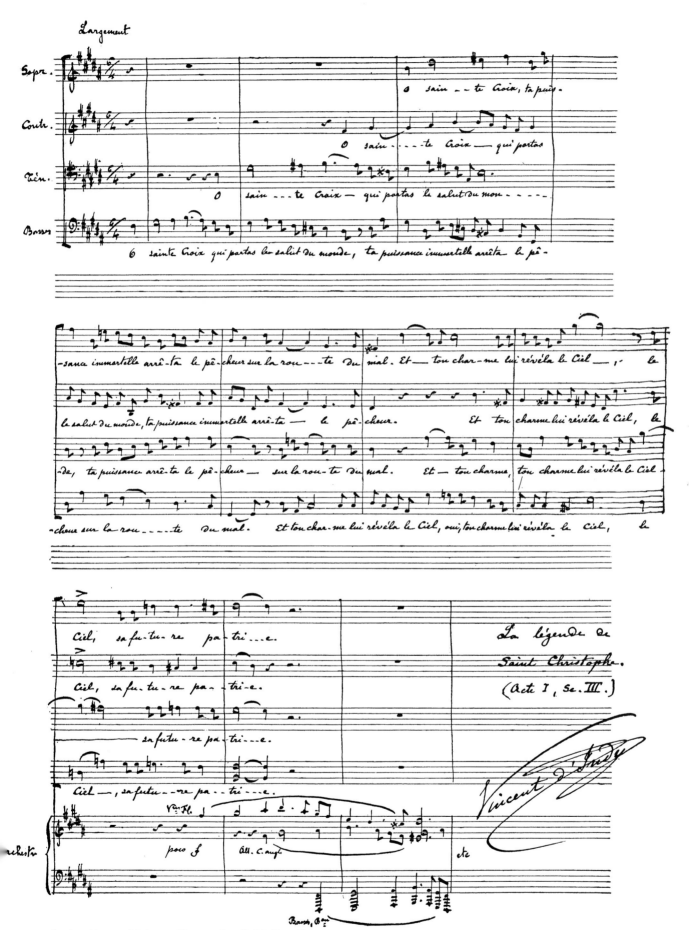

La partition est éditée par Rouart, Lerolle & Cie., Paris

II

PROSE

CONTRIBUTORS OF PROSE

MAURICE BARRÈS

SARAH BERNHARDT

PAUL BOURGET

JOSEPH CONRAD

ELEONORA DUSE

JOHN GALSWORTHY

EDMUND GOSSE

PAUL HERVIEU

GÉNÉRAL HUMBERT

HENRY JAMES

MAURICE MAETERLINCK

EDWARD SANDFORD MARTIN

PAUL ELMER MORE

AGNES REPPLIER

ANDRÉ SAURÈS

MRS. HUMPHRY WARD

LES FRÈRES

JE n'aime pas raconter cette histoire, dit le Général, parce que à chaque fois, c'est bête, je pleure. Mais elle fait aimer la France. . . . Il s'agit de deux enfants admirablement doués, pleins de cœur et d'esprit et qu'aimaient tous ceux qui les rencontraient. Je les avais connus tout petits. Quand la guerre éclata, le plus jeune, François, venait d'être admis à Saint-Cyr. Il n'eut pas le temps d'y entrer et avec toute la promotion il fut d'emblée nommé sous-lieutenant. Vous pensez s'il rayonnait de joie! Dix-neuf ans l'épaulette et les batailles! Son aîné Jacques, un garçon de vingt ans, tout à fait remarquable de science et d'éloquence, travaillait encore à la Faculté de Droit dont il était lauréat. Lui aussi il partit comme sous-lieutenant.

Les deux frères se retrouvèrent dans la même brigade de "la division de fer," le plus jeune au 26ᵉ de ligne et l'aîné au 27ᵉ. Ils cantonnaient dans un village dévasté et chaque jour joyeusement se retrouvaient, plaisant à tous et gagnant par leur jeunesse et leur amitié une sorte de popularité auprès des soldats.

Bientôt on apprit que le régiment du Saint-Cyrien allait avoir à marcher et que ce serait chaud. En cachette Jacques s'en alla demander au colonel la permission de prendre la place de son petit François qu'il trouvait trop peu préparé pour une action qui s'annonçait rude.

Le colonel reconnut la générosité de cette demande mais coupa court en disant:

—On ne peut pas faire passer un officier d'un corps à un autre corps.

Le jour fixé pour l'attaque arriva. La première compagnie à laquelle appartenait François fut envoyé en tirailleurs. Elle fut fauchée. Une autre suivit. Et puis une autre encore. Leurs ailes durent se replier en laissant sur le terrain leurs morts et une partie de leurs blessés. Le petit sous-lieutenant n'était pas de ceux qui revinrent.

Le surlendemain nous reprîmes l'offensive. L'aîné en enlevant avec son régiment les tranchées allemandes, passa auprès du corps de son petit François tout criblé de balles. Un peu plus loin il reçut une blessure à l'épaule.

Son capitaine lui ordonna d'aller se faire panser. Il refusa, continua et fut blessé d'une balle dans la tête.

Les corps furent ramassés et ramenés dans les ruines du village. Les sapeurs du 26ᵉ dirent alors:

—On n'enterrera pas ce bon petit sous-lieutenant sans un cercueil. Nous allons lui en faire un.

Ils se mirent à scier et à clouer.

Ceux du 27ᵉ dirent alors:

—Il ne faut pas traiter différemment les deux frères. Nous allons, nous aussi, faire un cercueil pour notre lieutenant.

Au soir, on se préparait à les enterrer côte à côte quand une vieille femme éleva la voix.

C'était une vieille si pauvre qu'elle avait obstinément refusé d'abandonner le village. "J'aime mieux mourir ici," avait-elle dit. On l'avait laissée. Elle gîtait misérablement dans sa cabane sur la paille et n'avait pas d'autre nourriture que celle que lui donnaient les soldats. Quand elle vit les deux jeunes cadavres et les préparatifs, elle dit:

—Attendez un instant avant de les enfermer. Je vais chercher quelque chose.

Elle alla fouiller la paille sur laquelle elle couchait et en tira le drap qu'elle gardait pour sa sépulture. Et revenant:

—On n'enfermera pas, dit-elle, ces beaux garçons le visage contre les planches. Je veux les ensevelir.

Elle coupa la toile en deux et les mit chacun dans son suaire, puis elle leur posa un baiser sur le front, en disant chaque fois:

—Pour la mère, mon cher enfant.

. . .

Nous nous tûmes quand le Général eut ainsi parlé et il n'était pas le seul à avoir des larmes dans les yeux. Une prière d'amour se formait dans nos cœurs pour la France.

MAURICE BARRÈS

de l'Académie Française

1915

THE BROTHERS

[TRANSLATION]

I'M not fond of telling this story, said the General, because each time, like the old fool I am, it brings tears to my eyes . . . but the best of France is in it.

It's about two boys, astonishingly gifted, full of heart and brains, that nobody could meet without liking. I knew them when they were tiny little fellows. At the time war broke out, the younger one, François, had just passed his examinations for St. Cyr. He had no time to enter; he was rushed along in the wholesale promotion and made second lieutenant then and there. Fancy what it meant to him — epaulettes and battles at nineteen! His elder brother, Jacques, a boy of twenty, — a really remarkable fellow in his studies, was hard at work in the Law School, where he had taken honors. He went off to the front as second lieutenant, too.

The two brothers were thrown together for the first time in the same brigade of the "iron division," as it was called — the younger in the 26th of the line, the other in the 27th. They were quartered in a ruined village, and each day they met, making themselves liked everywhere and enjoying a great popularity with the soldiers on account of their youth and friendliness.

It soon got round that the St. Cyr boy's regiment was going to get some hot fighting. Jacques said nothing, but he went to his colonel and asked for permission to take the place of his brother, whom he considered too little prepared for what promised to be a violent engagement.

The colonel recognized the generosity of this request, but he cut the young man short.

"An officer can't be transferred from his own corps to another," he said.

The day fixed for the attack came. The first company—François' company—was sent ahead to skirmish. It was simply mowed down. Another followed, and then another. They finally had to fall back, leaving their dead and part of the wounded on the field. The little second lieutenant was not among those who returned.

Two days later our men took the offensive again. The elder brother, storming the German trenches with his regiment, passed close by the body of his little François as it lay there all shot to pieces. A bit farther on, a bullet caught him in the shoulder.

His captain ordered him back to have the wound dressed; he refused, kept on, and was hit full in the forehead.

The bodies were taken up and carried back to the ruins of the village. The sappers of the 26th said:

"He was a fine fellow, that little second lieutenant. He shan't go underground without a coffin, at any rate. Let's make one for him."

And they began sawing and hammering.

Then the men of the 27th put their heads together and said:

"There must be no difference between the two brothers. We might as well make a coffin for our lieutenant, too."

By nightfall, when they were ready to bury the brothers side by side, an old woman spoke up. She was a wretched old creature, so poor and broken that she stubbornly refused to leave the village. "I've lived here, I'll die here," she kept on saying. She lay huddled up on some straw in her little hovel, and her only food was the leavings of the soldiers. When she saw the bodies of the two lads and understood what was going on, she said:

"Wait a minute before you nail the covers on. I'm going to fetch something."

MAURICE BARRÈS

She hobbled away, fumbled around in the straw she slept on, and pulled out a piece of cloth that she was keeping for her shroud.

"They shan't nail those boys up with their faces against the boards. I want to shroud them," she said.

She cut the shroud in two and wrapped each in a half of it. Then she kissed each one of them on the forehead, saying,

"That's for your mother, dearie."

. . .

No one spoke when the General ended. And he was not the only one to have wet eyes. In each of our hearts there was a prayer for France.

MAURICE BARRÈS
de l'Académie Française

1915

UNE PROMESSE

Séchez vos larmes, Enfants des Flandres!

Car les canons, les mitrailleuses, les fusils, les sabres et les bras n'arrêteront leur élan que lorsque l'ennemi vaincu vous rendra vos foyers!

Et ces foyers; nous, les femmes de France, d'Angleterre, de Russie et d'Italie, nous les ensoleillerons.

SARAH BERNHARDT

1915

A PROMISE

[TRANSLATION]

CHILDREN of Flanders, dry your tears!

For all the mighty machinery of war, and the stout hearts of brave men, shall strive together till the vanquished foe has given you back your homes!

And to those homes made desolate, we, the women of France, of England, of Russia and of Italy, will bring again happiness and sunlight!

SARAH BERNHARDT

PIERRE-AUGUSTE RÉNOIR

PORTRAIT OF HIS SON, WOUNDED IN THE WAR

FROM A CHARCOAL SKETCH

PAUL BOURGET

APRÉS UN AN

Je me trouvais, au début de ce mois d'août 1915, voyager en automobile dans une des provinces du centre de la France, que j'avais traversée de même, juste une année auparavant, quand la mobilisation commençante remplissait les routes de camions, de canons, de troupes en marche. Une année! Que de morts depuis! Mais la résolution demeure la même qu'à cette époque où le Pays tout entier n'eut qu'un mot d'ordre: y aller. Non. Rien n'a changé de cette volonté de bataille. J'entre dans un hôtel, pour y déjeuner. La patronne, que je connais pour m'arrêter là chaque fois que je passe par la petite ville, est entièrement vêtue de noir. Elle a perdu son frère en Alsace. Son mari est dans un dépôt à la veille de partir au front. "Faites-vous des affaires?" lui demandé-je. —"Pas beaucoup. Personne ne circule, et tous les mobilisés s'en vont. La caserne se vide. Encore ce matin—" — "C'est bien long," lui dis-je, pour la tenter. —"Oui, monsieur," répond-elle, "mais puisqu'il faut çà—" Et elle recommence d'écrire ses menus, sans une plainte. Dans la salle à manger, deux servantes, dont une aussi tout en noir. Je la questionne. Son mari a été tué sur l'Yser. Son visage est très triste. Mais pas une récrimination non plus. Elle est comme sa maîtresse. Elle accepte "puisqu'il faut çà." Un sous-officier ouvre la porte. Il est suivi d'une femme en grand deuil, d'un enfant et d'un homme âgé.—Sa femme, son fils et son père, ai-je su depuis. Je le vois de profil, et j'observe dans son regard une fixité qui m'étonne. Il refuse une place dans le fond, et marche vers la fenêtre: "J'ai besoin d'avoir plus de jour maintenant," répète-t-il, d'un accent singulier. A peine est-il assis avec sa famille, qu'un des convives de la table d'hôte, en train de déjeuner, se lève, et vient le saluer avec une exclamation de surprise. "Vous ici! Vous êtes donc debout? D'ailleurs, vous avez très belle mine."—"Oui," dit le sous-officier, "çà n'empêche pas qu'il est en verre—" Et il montre son œil droit. En quelques mots, très simplement, il raconte qu'une balle lui a enlevé cet œil droit en Argonne. "C'est dommage," continue-t-il, "on était si bien, si contents de n'être plus dans l'eau et dans la boue." Et l'autre de s'écrier: "Vous êtes tous comme çà, dans l'armée, si braves, si modestes! Nous autres, les vieux, nous n'avons été que de la Saint-Jean à côté de vous. 70, qu'est-ce que c'était? Rien du tout. Mais çà finira autrement."—"Il le faut," dit le sous-officier, "et pour nous, et pour ces pauvres Belges à qui nous devons d'avoir eu du temps. Oui," insiste-t-il, en posant sa main sur la tête de son enfant, "pour ceux-là aussi il le faut."—"Qui est ce monsieur?" dis-je à la servante.—"Ce sous-officier?" répond-elle, "un négociant de Paris. Le frère de sa dame a été tué." Je regarde manger ces gens, si éprouvés. Ils sont bien sérieux, bien accablés, mais si dignes. Les mots que ce borgne héroïque a prononcés, cet "il le faut" donne à tous leurs gestes une émouvante gravité.

Je reprends ma route, et je le retrouve cet "il le faut" du sergent, ce "puisqu'il faut çà" de l'hôtelière, comme écrit dans tous les aspects de cet horizon. C'est le moment de la moisson. Des femmes y travaillent, des garçonnets, des petites filles. La suppléance du mari, du père, du frère absents, s'est faite simplement, sans qu'il y ait eu besoin d'aucun appel, d'aucun décret. Sur deux charrettes que je croise, une est menée par une femme. Des femmes conduisent les troupeaux. Des femmes étaient derrière les guichets de la Banque où je suis descendu chercher de la monnaie, dans la petite ville. Un de mes amis, qui a de gros intérêts dans le midi, me racontait que son homme d'affaires est aux Dardanelles: "Sa femme gère mes propriétés à sa place. Elle est étonnante d'intelligence et de bravoure." Oui, c'est toujours ce même tranquille stoïcisme, cette totale absence de plainte. Un bataillon de territoriaux défile. Ils ne sont plus jeunes. Leur existence était établie. Elle est bouleversée. Ils subissent l'épreuve sans un murmure et marquent le pas sur la route brûlée de soleil avec une énergie qui révèle, chez eux aussi, le sentiment de la nécessité. C'est, pour moi, le caractère pathétique de cette guerre. Elle a la grandeur auguste des actions vitales de la nature. Elle est le geste d'un pays qui ne veut pas mourir, et qui ne mourra pas, ni lui ni cette noble

PAUL BOURGET

Belgique, dont parlait le sous-officier, et qui, elle, a prononcé avec autant de fermeté résolue son "il le faut," quand l'Allemand l'a provoquée, et plus pathétiquement encore. Ce n'était pas pour la vie qu'elle allait se battre, c'était pour l'honneur, pour la probité. Il n'est pas un Français qui ne le sente, et qui ne confonde sa propre cause avec celle des admirables sujets de l'admirable Roi Albert.

PAUL BOURGET
de l'Académie Française

ONE YEAR LATER

[TRANSLATION]

DURING the first days of August, 1915, I found myself motoring in one of the central provinces of France. I had crossed the same region in the same way just a year before, when the beginning of mobilization was crowding the roads with waggons, with artillery and with marching troops. Only one year! How many men are dead since! But the high resolve of the nation is as firm as it was then, when all through the land there was only one impulse—to go forward. The willingness to fight and to endure has not grown less.

I went into an hotel for luncheon. I know the woman who keeps it, because I always stop there when I go through the little town. I found her dressed in black: she had lost her brother in Alsace. Her husband was waiting to be sent to the front. I asked her if she were doing any business. "Not much," she answered. "Nobody is travelling, and all the mobilized men are gone. The barracks are empty; why, only this morning—" "It seems a long time," I said, to draw her on. "Yes," she said, "but since we must..." and she went back without complaint to the task of writing her bills of fare. There were two maids in the dining-room, one of them also in black. I questioned her and learnt that her husband had been killed on the Yser. Her face was full of sorrow, but like her mistress she blamed no one, and accepted her loss because it "must" be so.

Soon a non-commissioned officer came in, followed by a woman in deep mourning, a little boy, and an elderly man; I learnt afterwards that they were the sergeant's wife, his son, and his father. I saw his profile, and noticed that he seemed to stare fixedly. He declined a place at the back of the room, and came toward the window. "I need plenty of light now," he said in an odd voice. He and his family had just seated themselves when one of the guests at the long *table d'hôte* rose with an exclamation of surprise and came over to him, saying: "Why, are you out again? How well you look!" "Yes," said the sergeant; "but all the same this one is glass," pointing to his right eye, and in a few words he told how it had been knocked out by a bullet in the Argonne. "It was such a pity," he said, "for we were all so glad when the fighting began, and we got out of the mud and water in the trenches." "You are all just like that in the army!" said his friend, "all so plucky and so simple! We old fellows were only amateurs compared to you! What was the war of 1870 to this one? This time there will be a different ending." "There must be," said the sergeant, "not only for us but for the Belgians, who gained us so much time." And he repeated, laying his hand on his boy's head, "Yes, for these little chaps also it must be so."

Presently I found a chance to ask the maid what she knew about the soldier who had been speaking. "That sergeant? He is a Paris shopkeeper. His wife's brother has been killed." I watched these people at table, so serious, so sorely tried, but so full of dignity, and the words which the half-blinded man had pronounced seemed to make even his ordinary gestures impressive.

All along the road, for the rest of that journey the "it must be" of the hotel-keeper and the sergeant seemed to be written over the whole country-side. It was harvest-time, and women, lads and little girls were working in the fields, replacing absent husbands, fathers and brothers.

PAUL BOURGET

They were doing it quite simply, not drawn by any appeal, nor compelled by any order. Every other cart I met was driven by a woman. Women were herding the cattle. There was a woman at the cashier's desk of the bank in the town where I went to get some money changed.

One of my friends, who has large interests in the south of France, told me that his man of business was at the Dardanelles. "His wife looks after my property in his place. She is astonishingly intelligent and capable." Everywhere the same tranquil stoicism, the same entire absence of complaint.

A battalion of territorials marched past. They were not young men. All of them had had fixed duties and habits which were now broken up. Yet they submitted without a murmur, marching along the hot and dusty road with an energy which revealed in them also the same sense of compelling necessity. That, to my mind, gives to this war its pathetic side. It has all the imposing grandeur of the vital forces of nature; it is the heroic movement of a country which defies death, which is not meant to die. Nor will she allow Belgium to die—the Belgium to whom the sergeant paid his tribute, and whose "we must" rang out with such poignant firmness under the German menace. It was not for life alone that Belgium fought, but for honour and for justice. No Frenchman lives who does not feel this, and who does not merge his own cause in that of the indomitable subjects of Belgium's indomitable King.

PAUL BOURGET
de l'Académie Française

LÉON BONNAT

PEGASUS

à Madame Wharton
hommage très respectueux,

R. W. Bornal

JOSEPH CONRAD

POLAND REVISITED

I

I HAVE never believed in political assassination as a means to an end, and least of all if the assassination is of the dynastic order. I don't know how far murder can ever approach the efficiency of a fine art, but looked upon with the cold eye of reason it seems but a crude expedient either of impatient hope or hurried despair. There are few men whose premature death could influence human affairs more than on the surface. The deeper stream of causes depends not on individualities which, like the mass of mankind, are carried on by the destiny which no murder had ever been able to placate, divert or arrest.

In July of [1914] I was a stranger in a strange city and particularly out of touch with the world's politics. Never a very diligent reader of newspapers, there were at that time reasons of a private order which caused me to be even less informed than usual on public affairs as presented from day to day in that particular atmosphere-less, perspective-lessness of the daily papers which somehow for a man with some historic sense robs them of all real interest. I don't think I had looked at a daily for a month past.

But though a stranger in a strange city I was not lonely, thanks to a friend who had travelled there with me out of pure kindness, to bear me company in a conjuncture which, in a most private sense, was somewhat trying.

It was this friend who one morning at breakfast informed me of the murder of the Archduke Ferdinand.

The impression was mediocre. I was barely aware that such a man existed. I remembered only that not long before he had visited London, but that memory was lost in a cloud of insignificant printed words his presence in this country provoked. Various opinions had been expressed of him, but his importance had been archducal, dynastic, purely accidental. Can there be in the world of real men anything more shadowy than an archduke? And now he was no more, and with a certain atrocity of circumstance which made one more sensible of his humanity than when he was in life. I knew nothing of his journey. I did not connect that crime with Balkanic plots and aspirations. I asked where it had happened. My friend told me it was in Serajevo, and wondered what would be the consequences of that grave event. He asked me what I thought would happen next.

It was with perfect sincerity that I said "Nothing," and I dismissed the subject, having a great repugnance to consider murder as an engine of politics. It fitted with my ethical sense that an act cruel and absurd should be also useless. I had also the vision of a crowd of shadowy archdukes in the background out of which one would step forward to take the place of that dead man in the sun of European politics. And then, to speak the whole truth, there was no man capable of forming a judgement who attended so little to the march of events as I did at that time. What for want of a more definite term I must call my mind was fixed on my own affairs, not because they were in a bad posture, but because of their fascinating, holiday promising aspect. I obtained my information as to Europe at second hand, from friends good enough to come down now and then to see us with their pockets full of crumpled papers, and who imparted it to me casually with gentle smiles of scepticism as to the reality of my interest. And yet I was not indifferent; but the tension in the Balkans had become chronic after the acute crisis, and one could not help being less conscious of it. It had wearied out one's attention. Who could have guessed that on that wild stage we had just been looking at a miniature rehearsal of the great world drama, the reduced model of the very passions and violences of what the future held in store for the powers of the Old World? Here and there, perhaps, rare minds had a suspicion of that possibility while watching the collective Europe stage managing a little contemptuously in a feeling of conscious superiority, by means of notes and conferences, the prophetic reproduction of its awaiting fate. It was wonderfully exact in the spirit, same roar of guns, same protestations of superiority, same words in the air: race, liberation, justice, and the same mood of trivial demonstration. You could not take to-day a ticket for Petersburg, however roundabout the route. "You mean Petrograd," would say the booking-clerk. Shortly after the fall of Adrianople a friend of mine passing through Sophia asked for some " café turc" at the end of his lunch.

—"Monsieur veut dire café balkanique," the patriotic waiter corrected him austerely.

I will not say that I had not seen something of that instructive aspect in the war of the Balkans, both in its first and even in its second phase. But those with whom I touched upon that vision were pleased to see in it the evidence of an alarmist cynicism. As to alarm I pointed out that fear is natural to man and even salutary. It has done as much as courage for the preservation of races and institutions. But from a charge of cynicism I have always shrunk instinctively. It is like a charge of being blind in one eye, a moral disablement, a sort of disgraceful calamity that must be carried off by a jaunty bearing—a sort of thing I am not capable of. Rather than be thought to be a mere jaunty cripple I allowed myself to be blinded by the gross obviousness of the usual arguments. It had been pointed out to me that those were nations not far removed from a savage state. Their economics were yet at the stage of scratching the earth and feeding pigs. The complex material civilization of Europe could not allow itself to be disturbed by war. The industry and the finance could not allow themselves to be disorganised by the ambitions of the idle class or even the aspirations, whatever they might be, of the masses.

Very plausible all this sounded. War does not pay. There had been even a book written on that theme—an attempt to put pacifism on a material basis. Nothing more solid could have been imagined on this trading and manufacturing globe. War was bad business! This was final.

But truth to say on this fateful July I reflected but little on the condition of the civilised world. Whatever sinister passions were heaving under its splendid and complex surface, I was too agitated by a simple and innocent desire to notice the signs, or to interpret them correctly. The most innocent of passions takes the edge off one's judgement. The desire which obsessed me was simply the desire of travel. And that being so, it would have taken something very plain in the way of symptoms to shake my simple trust in the stability of things on the continent. My sentiment and not my reason was engaged there. My eyes were turned to the past, not to the future—the past that one cannot suspect and mistrust, the shadowy and unquestionable moral possession, the darkest struggles of which wear a halo of glory and peace.

In the preceding month of May we had received an invitation to spend some weeks in Poland in a country house in the neighbourhood of Cracow but on the other side of the Russian frontier. The enterprise at first seemed to be considerable. Since leaving the sea to which I have been faithful for so many years, I have discovered that there is in my composition very little stuff from which travellers are made. I confess it with shame, my first idea about a projected journey is to leave it alone.

But that invitation, received at first with a sort of uneasiness, awoke the dormant energies in my feelings. Cracow is the town where I spent with my father the last eighteen months of his life. It was in that old royal and academical city that I ceased to be a child, became a boy, knew the friendships, the admirations, the thoughts and the indignation of that age. It was between those historic walls that I began to understand things, form affections, lay up a store of memories and a fund of sensations with which I was to break violently by throwing myself into an unrelated life which permitted me but seldom to look back that way. The wings of time were spread over all this, and I feared at first that if I ventured bodily in there I would find that I who have evoked so many imaginary lives had been embracing mere shadows in my youth. I feared. But fear in itself may become a fascination. Men have gone alone, trembling, into graveyards at midnight—just to see what would happen. And this adventure was to be pursued in sunshine. Neither would it be pursued alone. The invitation was extended to us all. This journey would have something of a migratory character, the invasion of a tribe. My present, all that gave solidity and value to it at any rate, would stand by me in this test of the reality of my past. I was pleased to show my companions what Polish country life was like and the town where I was at school, before my boys got too old, and gaining an individual past of their own should lose the fresh sympathies of their age. It is only in this short understanding of youth that perhaps we have the faculty of coming out of ourselves to see dimly the visions and share the trouble of another soul. For youth all is reality, and with justice; since they can apprehend so vividly its images behind which a longer life makes one doubt whether there is any substance. I trusted to the fresh receptivity of these young beings in whom, unless heredity is merely a phantasy, there should have been fibre which would quicken at the sight, the atmosphere, the memories, of that corner of the earth where my own boyhood received its first independent impressions.

The first of the third week in July, while the telegraph wires hummed with the words of enormous import which were to fill blue-books, yellow-books, white-books and rouse the wonder of the world, was taken up with light-hearted preparation for the journey. What was it but just a rush through Germany to get over as quickly as possible?

It is the part of the earth's solid surface of which I know the least. In my life I had been across it only twice. I may well say of it, "Vidi tantum," and that very little I saw through the window of a railway carriage at express speed. Those journeys were more like pilgrimages when one hurries on towards the goal without looking to the right or left for the satisfaction of deeper need than curiosity. In this last instance, too, I was so uncurious that I would have liked to fall asleep on the shores of England and open my eyes only, if it were possible, on the other side of the Silesian frontier.

Yet in truth, as many others have done, I had "sensed it," that promised land of steel, of chemical dyes, of method, of efficiency; that race planted in the middle of Europe, assuming in grotesque vanity the attitude of Europeans amongst effete Asiatics or mere niggers, and with a feeling of superiority freeing their hands of all moral bonds and anxious to take up, if I may express myself so, the "perfect man's burden." Meantime in a clearing of the Teutonic forest their sages were rearing a Tree of cynical wisdom, a sort of Upas tree, whose shade may be seen lying now over the prostrate body of Belgium. It must be said that they laboured open enough, watering it from the most authentic sources of all evil, and watching with bespectacled eyes the slow ripening of the glorious blood-red fruit. The sincerest words of peace, words of menace, and I verily believe, words of abasement even, if there had been a voice vile enough to utter them, would have been wasted on their ecstasy. For when a fruit ripens on a branch, it must fall. There is nothing on earth that can prevent it.

II

For reasons which at first seemed to me somewhat obscure, that one of my companions whose wishes are law decided that our travels should begin in an unusual way by the crossing of the North Sea. We should proceed from Harwich to Hamburg. Besides being thirty-six times longer than the usual Dover-Calais passage this rather unusual route had an air of adventure in better keeping with the romantic feeling of this Polish journey, which for so many years had been before us in a state of a project full of colour and promise, but always retreating, elusive, like an enticing mirage.

And, after all, it had turned out to be no mirage. No wonder they were excited. It's no mean experience to lay your hands on a mirage. The day of departure had come, the very hour had struck. The luggage was coming downstairs. It was most convincing. Poland then, if erased from the map, yet existed in reality; it was not a mere "pays du rêve," where you can travel only in imagination. For no man, they argued, not even father, an habitual pursuer of dreams, would push the love of the novelist's art of make-believe to the point of burdening himself with real trunks for a voyage "au pays du rêve."

As we left the door of our house, nestling in, perhaps, the most peaceful nook in Kent, the sky, after weeks of perfectly brazen serenity, veiled its blue depths and started to weep fine tears for the refreshment of the parched fields. A pearly blurr settled over them; a light sifted of all glare, of everything unkindly and searching that dwells in the splendour of unveiled skies. All unconscious of going towards the very scenes of war, I carried off in my eye this tiny fragment of Great Britain: a few fields, a wooded rise, a clump of trees or two, with a short stretch of road, and here and there a gleam of red wall and tiled roof above the darkening hedges wrapped up in soft mist and peace. And I felt that all this had a very strong hold on me as the embodiment of a beneficent and gentle spirit; that it was dear to me not as an inheritance, but as an acquisition, as a conquest in the sense in which a woman is conquered—by love, which is a sort of surrender.

Those were strange, as if disproportionate thoughts to the matter in hand, which was the simplest sort of a Continental holiday. And I am certain that my companions, near as they are to me, felt no other trouble but the suppressed excitement of pleasurable anticipation. The forms and the spirit of the land before their eyes were their inheritance, not their conquest—which is a thing precarious, and, therefore, the more precious, possessing you if only by the fear of unworthiness, rather than possessed by you. Moreover, as we sat together in the same railway carriage, they were looking forward to a voyage in space, whereas I felt more and more plainly that what I had started on was a journey in time, into the past; a fearful enough prospect for the most consistent, but to him who had not known how to preserve against his impulses the order and continuity of his life—so that at times it presented itself to his conscience as a series of betrayals—still more dreadful.

I confess here my thoughts so exclusively personal to explain why there was no room in my consciousness for the apprehension of a European war. I don't mean to say I ignored the possibility. I simply did not think of it. And it made no difference; for, if I had thought of it, it could only have been in the lame and inconclusive way of the common unin-itiated mortals; and I am sure that nothing short of intellectual certitude —obviously unattainable by the man in the street—could have stayed me on that journey which now that I had started on it seemed an irre-vocable thing, a necessity of my self-respect.

London—the London of before the war, flaunting its enormous glare as of a monstrous conflagration up into the black sky—received us with its best Venice-like aspect of rainy evenings, the wet, asphalted streets lying with the sheen of sleeping water in winding canals, and the great houses of the city towering all dark like empty palaces above the re-flected lights of the glistening roadway.

Everything in the subdued incomplete night life around the Mansion House went on normally, with its fascinating air of a dead commercial city of sombre walls through which the inextinguishable night life of millions streamed East and West in a brilliant flow of lighted vehicles.

In Liverpool Street, as usual too, through the double gates, a contin-uous line of taxicabs glided down the inclined approach and up again, like an endless chain of dredger-buckets pouring in the passengers, and dipping them out of the great railway station under the inexorable pallid face of the clock telling off the diminishing minutes of peace. It was the hour of the boat trains to Holland, to Hamburg, and there seemed to be no lack of people, fearless, reckless, or ignorant, who wanted to go to these places. The station was normally crowded, and if there was a great flutter of evening papers in the multitude of hands, there were no signs of extraordinary emotion on that multitude of faces. There was nothing in them to distract me from the thought that it was singularly appropri-ate that I should start from this station on the retraced way of my exist-ence. For this was the station at which, thirty-six years ago, I arrived on my first visit to London. Not the same building, but the same spot. At eighteen years of age, after a period of probation and training I had imposed upon myself as ordinary seaman on board a North Sea coaster, I had come up from Lowestoft—my first long railway journey in England—to "sign on" for an Antipodean voyage in a deep-water ship. Straight from a railway carriage I had walked into the great city with something of the feeling of a traveller penetrating into a vast and unexplored wilderness. No explorer could have been more lonely. I did not know a single soul of all these millions that all around me peopled the mysterious distances of the streets. I cannot say I was free from a little youthful awe, but at that age one's feelings are simple. I was elated. I was pursuing a clear aim. I was carrying out a deliberate plan of making out of myself, in the first place, a seaman worthy of the service, good enough to work by the side of the men with whom I was to live; and in the second place, I had to justify my existence to myself, to redeem a tacit moral pledge. Both these aims were to be attained by the same effort. How simple seemed the problem of life then, on that hazy day of early September in the year 1878, when I entered London for the first time.

From that point of view—youth and a straightforward scheme of conduct—it was certainly a year of grace. All the help I had to get in touch with the world I was invading was a piece of paper not much bigger than the palm of my hand—in which I held it—torn out of a larger plan of London for the greater facility of reference. It had been the object of careful study for some days past. The fact that I could take a conveyance at the station had never occurred to my mind, no, not even when I got out into the street and stood, taking my anxious bearings, in the midst, so to speak, of twenty thousand cabs. A strange absence of mind or unconscious conviction that one cannot approach an important moment of one's life by means of a hired carriage? Yes, it would have been a preposterous proceeding. And indeed I was to make an Australian voyage and encircle the globe before ever entering a London hansom.

Another document, a cutting from a newspaper, containing the address of an obscure agent, was in my pocket. And I needed not to take it out.

That address was as if graven deep in my brain. I muttered its words to myself as I walked on, navigating the sea of London by the chart concealed in the palm of my hand; for I had vowed to myself not to inquire my way from any one. Youth is the time of rash pledges. Had I taken a wrong turn I would have been lost; and if faithful to my pledge I might have remained lost for days, for weeks, have left perhaps my bones to be discovered bleaching in some blind alley of the Whitechapel district, as had happened to lonely travellers lost in the bush. But I walked on to my destination without hesitation or mistake, showing there, for the first time, something of that faculty to absorb and make my own correctly the imaged topography of a chart, which in later years was to help me in regions of intricate navigation to keep the ships entrusted to me off the ground. And the place I was bound to was not so easy to find, either. It was one of those courts hidden away from the charted and navigable streets, lost amongst the thick growth of houses, like a dark pool in the depths of a forest, approached by an inconspicuous archway, as if by a secret path; a Dickensian nook of London, that wonder-city, the growth of which bears no sign of intelligent design, but many traces of freakishly sombre phantasy which the great Master knew so well how to bring out by magic of his great and understanding love. And the office I entered was Dickensian too. The dust of the Waterloo year lay on the panes and frames of its windows; early Georgian grime clung to its sombre wainscoting.

It was one o'clock in the afternoon, but the day was gloomy. By the light of a single gas-jet depending from the smoked ceiling I saw an elderly man, in a long coat of black broadcloth. He had a grey beard, a big nose, thick lips, and broad shoulders. His longish white hair and the general character of his head recalled vaguely a burly apostle in the "barocco" style of Italian art. Standing up at a tall, shabby, slanting desk, his silver-rimmed spectacles pushed up high on his forehead, he was eating a mutton chop, which had been just brought to him from some Dickensian eating-house round the corner.

Without ceasing to eat he turned to me his barocco apostle's head with an expression of inquiry.

I produced elaborately a series of vocal sounds which must have borne sufficient resemblance to the phonetics of English speech; for his face broke into a smile of comprehension almost at once.—"Oh it's you who wrote a letter to me the other day from Lowestoft about getting a ship."

I had written to him from Lowestoft. I can't remember a single word of that letter now. It was my very first composition in the English language. And he had understood it; because he spoke to the point at once, explaining that his business, mainly, was to find good ships for young gentlemen who wanted to go to sea as premium apprentices with a view of being trained for officers. But he gathered that this was not my object. I did not desire to be apprenticed. Was that the case?

It was. He was good enough to say then, "Of course I see that you are a gentleman too. But your wish is to get a berth before the mast as an Able Seaman if possible. Is that it?"

It was certainly my wish; but he stated doubtfully that he feared he could not help me much in this. There was an Act of Parliament which made it penal to procure ships for sailors. "An Act—of—Parliament. A law," he took pains to impress it again and again on my foreign understanding, while I looked at him in consternation.

I had not been half an hour in London before I had run my head against an Act of Parliament! What a hopeless adventure! However, the barocco apostle was a resourceful person in his way, and we managed to get round the hard letter of it without damage to its fine spirit. Yet, strictly speaking, it was not the conduct of a good citizen. And in retrospect there is an unfilial flavour about that early sin. For this Act of Parliament, the Merchant Shipping Act of the mid-Victorian era, had been in a manner of speaking a father and mother to me. For many years it had regulated and disciplined my life, prescribed my food and the amount of my breathing space, had looked after my health and tried as much as possible to secure my personal safety in a risky calling. It isn't such a bad thing to lead a life of hard toil and plain duty within the four corners of an honest Act of Parliament. And I am glad to say that its severities have never been applied to me.

In the year 1878, the year of Peace with Honour, I had walked as lone as any human being in the streets of London, out of Liverpool Street Station, to surrender myself to its care. And now, in the year of the war waged for honour and conscience more than for any other cause, I was there again, no longer alone, but a man of infinitely dear and close ties grown since that time, of work done, of words written, of friendship secured. It was like the closing of a thirty-six years' cycle.

All unaware of the War Angel already waiting with the trumpet at its lips the stroke of the fatal hour, I sat there, thinking that this life of ours is neither long nor short, but that it can appear very wonderful, entertaining, and pathetic, with symbolic images and bizarre associations crowded into one half-hour of retrospective musing.

I felt, too, that this journey so suddenly entered upon was bound to take me away from daily life's actualities at every step. I felt it more than ever when presently we steamed out into the North Sea, on a dark night fitful with gusts of wind, and I lingered on deck, alone of all the tale of the ship's passengers. That sea was to me something unforgettable, something much more than a name. It had been for a time the school-room of my trade. On it, I may safely say, I had learned, too, my first words of English. A wild and stormy abode, sometimes, was that fine, narrow-waters academy of seamanship from which I launched myself on the wide oceans. My teachers had been the coasting sailors of the Norfolk shore. Coast men, with steady eyes, mighty limbs, and gentle voice. Men of very few words, which, at least, were never bare of meaning. Honest, strong, steady men, sobered by domestic ties, one and all as far as I can remember.

That is what years ago the North Sea, I could hear growling in the dark all round the ship, had been for me. And I fancied that I must have been carrying its voice in my ear ever since, for nothing could be more familiar than those short, angry sounds I was listening to with a smile of affectionate recognition.

I could not guess that before many days my schoolroom would be desecrated by violence, littered with wrecks, with death walking its waves, hiding under the waters. Perhaps while I am writing these words the children, or maybe the grandchildren, of my pacific teachers are out in drifters under the naval flag, dredging for German submarine mines.

III

I have said that the North Sea was my finishing school of seamanship before I launched myself on the wider oceans. Confined as it is in comparison with the vast stage of this water-girt globe, I did not know it in all its parts. My classroom was the region of the English East Coast which, in the year of Peace with Honour, had long forgotten the war episodes belonging to its maritime history. It was a peaceful coast, agricultural, industrial, the home of fishermen. At night the lights of its many towns played on the clouds, or in clear weather lay still, here and there, in brilliant pools above the ink-black outline of the shore. On many a night I have hauled at the braces under the very shadow of that coast, envying, as sailors will, the people ashore sleeping quietly in their beds within sound of the sea. I imagine that not one head on these envied pillows was made uneasy by the slightest premonition of the realities of naval war the short lifetime of one generation was to bring to their peaceful shores.

Though far away from that region of kindly memories and traversing a part of the North Sea much less known to me, I was deeply conscious of the familiarity of my surroundings. It was a cloudy, nasty day, and the aspects of nature don't change, unless in the course of thousands of years—or, perhaps, centuries. The Phœnicians, its first discoverers, the Romans, the first imperial rulers of that sea, had experienced days like this, so different in the wintry quality of the light even on that July afternoon, from anything they had ever known in their native Mediterranean. For myself, a very late comer into that sea and its former pupil, I accorded amused recognition to the characteristic aspect so well remembered from my days of training. The same old thing. A grey-green expanse of smudgy waters grinning angrily at one with white foam-ridges, and over all a cheerless, unglowing canopy, apparently made of wet blotting-paper. From time to time a flurry of fine rain blew along like a puff of smoke across the dots of distant fishing boats, very few, very scattered, very solid and motionless against an ever dissolving, ever re-forming sky-line.

Those flurries, and the steady rolling of the ship, accounted for the emptiness of the decks favouring my reminiscent mood.

It might have been a day of five-and-thirty years ago, when there was on this and every other sea more sails and less smoke-stacks to be seen. Yet, thanks to the unchangeable sea, I could have given myself up to the illusion bringing the past close to the future, if it had not been for the periodical transit across my gaze of a German passenger. He was marching round and round the boat-deck with characteristic determination. Two sturdy boys gambolled round him in his progress like two small disorderly satellites round their parent planet. He was bringing them home from their school in England for their holiday. What could have induced him to entrust his offspring to the unhealthy influences of that effete, corrupt, rotten and criminal country, I cannot imagine. It could hardly have been from motives of economy. I did not speak to him. He trod the deck of that decadent British ship with a scornful foot, while his breast (and to some extent his stomach, too) appeared expanded by the consciousness of a superior destiny. Later, I could observe the same truculent bearing, touched with the racial grotesqueness, in the men of the Landwehr corps, the first that passed through Cracow to reinforce the Austrian Army in Eastern Galicia. Indeed, the haughty passenger might very well have been, most probably was, an officer of the Landwehr; and perhaps those two fine, active boys are orphans by now. Thus things acquire significance by the lapse of time. A citizen, a father, a warrior, a mote in the dust-cloud of six million of fighting particles, still tossed East or West in the lurid tempest, or already snapped up, an unconsidered trifle, in the jaws of war, his very humanity was not consciously impressed on my mind at the time. Mainly, for me, he was a sharp tapping of heels round the corner of the deck-house, a white yachting-cap and a green overcoat getting periodically between my eyes and the shifting cloud-horizon of the ashy-green North Sea. He was but a shadowy intrusion and a disregarded one, for far away there to the West, in the direction of the Dogger Bank, where fishermen go seeking their daily bread and sometimes find their graves, I could behold an experience of my own in the winter of 1881, not of war truly, but of a fairly lively contest with the elements which were very angry indeed.

There had been a troublesome week of it, including one hateful night—or a night of hate (it is n't for nothing that the North Sea is also called the German Ocean)—when all the fury stored in its heart seemed concentrated on one ship which could do no better than to float on her side in an unnatural, disagreeable, precarious, and altogether intolerable manner. There were on board besides myself, seventeen men, all good and true, including a round enormous Dutchman who, in those hours between sunset and sunrise, managed to lose his blown-out appearance somehow, became as it were deflated, and thereafter for a long time moved in our midst wrinkled and slack all over like a half-collapsed balloon. The whimpering of our deck-boy, a skinny, impressionable little scarecrow out of a training-ship, for whom, because of the tender immaturity of his nerves, this display of German Ocean frightfulness was too much (before the year was out he developed into a sufficiently cheeky young ruffian), his desolate whimpering, I say, heard between the gusts of that black, savage night, was much more present to my mind and indeed to my senses, than the green overcoat and the white cap of the German passenger circling the deck indefatigably, attended by his two gyrating children.

"That's a very nice gentleman." This information, together with the fact that he was a widower and a regular passenger twice a year by the ship, was communicated to me suddenly by our captain. At intervals through the day he would pop out of his cabin and offer me short snatches of conversation. He owned a simple soul and a not very entertaining mind, and he was, without malice and, I believe, quite unconsciously, a warm Germanophil. And no wonder! As he told me himself, he had been fifteen years on that run, and spent almost as much of his life in Germany as in England.

"Wonderful people they are," he repeated from time to time, without entering into particulars, but with many nods of sagacious obstinacy. What he knew of them, I suppose, were a few commercial travellers and small merchants, most likely. But I had observed long before that German genius has a hypnotising power over half-baked souls and half-lighted minds. There is an immense force of suggestion in highly organised mediocrity. Had it not hypnotised half Europe? My man was very much under the spell of German excellence. On the other hand, his contempt for France was equally general and unbounded. I tried to advance some arguments against this position, but I only succeeded in making him hostile to myself. "I believe you are a Frenchman yourself," he snarled at last, giving me an intensely suspicious look; and forthwith broke off communications with a man of such unsound sympathies.

Hour by hour the blotting-paper sky and the great flat greenish smudge of the sea had been taking on a darker tone, without any change in their colouring and texture. Evening was coming on over the North Sea. Black uninteresting hummocks of land appeared, dotting the duskiness of water and clouds in the eastern board; tops of islands fringing the German shore. While I was looking at their antics amongst the waves—and for all their manifest solidity they were very elusive things in the failing light—another passenger came out on deck. This one wore a dark overcoat and a grey cap. The yellow leather strap of his binocular-case crossed his chest. His elderly red cheeks nourished but a very thin crop of short white hairs, and the end of his nose was so perfectly round that it determined the whole character of his physiognomy. Indeed, nothing else in it had the slightest chance to assert itself. His disposition, unlike the widower's, appeared to be mild and humane. He offered me the loan of his glasses. He had a wife and some small children concealed in the depths of the ship, and he thought that they were very well where they were. His eldest son was about the decks somewhere.

"We are Americans," he remarked weightily, but in a rather peculiar tone. He spoke English with the accent of our captain's "wonderful people," and proceeded to give me the history of the family's crossing the Atlantic in a White Star ship. They remained in England just the time necessary for a railway journey from Liverpool to Harwich. His people (those in the depths of the ship, I suppose) were naturally a little tired.

At that moment a young man of about twenty, his son, rushed up to us from the fore-deck in a state of intense elation. "Hurrah!" he cried under his breath, "The first German light! Hurrah!"

And those two American citizens shook hands on it with the greatest fervour, while I turned away and received full in the eyes the brilliant wink of the Borkum lighthouse squatting low down in the darkness. The shade of the night had settled on the North Sea.

I do not think I have ever seen before a night so full of lights. The great change of sea-life since my time was brought home to me. I had been conscious all day of an interminable procession of steamers. They went on and on as if in chase of each other, the Baltic trade, the trade of Scandinavia, of Denmark, of Germany, pitching heavily into a head-sea and bound for the gateway of Dover Strait. Singly, and in small companies of two or three, they emerged from the dull, colourless, sunless distances ahead, as if the supply of rather roughly finished mechanical toys were inexhaustible in some mysterious cheap store, away there, below the grey curve of the earth. Cargo steam-vessels have reached by this time a height of utilitarian ugliness which, when one reflects that this is the product of human ingenuity, strikes hopeless awe into one. These dismal creations look still uglier at sea than in port, and with an added touch of the ridiculous. Their rolling waddle when seen at a certain angle, their abrupt clockwork nodding in a seaway, so unlike the soaring lift and swing of a craft under sail, have in them something caricatural, a suggestion of low parody directed at noble predecessors by an improved generation of dull, mechanical toilers, conceited and without grace.

When they switched on (each of these unlovely cargo-tanks carried tame lightning within its slab-sided body), when they switched on their lamps they spangled the night with the cheap, electric, shop-glitter, here, there, and everywhere, as of some High Street, broken up and washed out to sea. Later, Heligoland cut into the overhead darkness with its powerful beam, infinitely prolonged out of unfathomable night under the clouds.

I remained on deck till we stopped and a steam pilot-boat, so over-lighted amidships that one could not make out her complete shape, glided across our bows and sent a pilot on board. I fear that the oar, as a working implement, shall become presently as obsolete as the sail. The pilot boarded us in a motor dinghy. More and more is mankind reducing its physical activities to pulling levers and twirling little wheels. Progress! Yet the older methods of meeting natural forces demanded intelligence too; an equally fine readiness of wits. And readiness of wits working in combination with the strength of muscles made a more complete man.

It was really a surprisingly small dinghy, and it ran to and fro like a water-insect fussing noisily down there with immense self-importance. Within hail of us the hull of the Elbe Lightship floated all dark and silent under its enormous, round, service lantern; a faithful black shadow watching the broad estuary full of lights.

Such was my first view of the Elbe approached under the wings of peace already spread for a flight away from the luckless shores of Europe. Our visual impressions remain with us so persistently that I find it extremely difficult to hold fast to the rational belief that now everything is dark over there, that the Elbe Lightship has been towed away from its post of duty, the triumphant beam of Heligoland extinguished, and

[88]

the pilot-boat laid up, or turned to warlike uses for lack of its proper work to do. And obviously it must be so.

Any trickle of oversea trade that passes yet that way must be creeping along cautiously, with the unlighted, war-blighted, black coast close on one, and sudden death on the other hand. For all the space we steamed through on that Sunday evening must be now one great mine field, sown thickly with the seeds of hate; while submarines steal out to sea, over the very spot, perhaps, where the insect-dinghy put a pilot on board of us with so much fussy importance. Mines, submarines. The last word in sea warfare! Progress—impressively disclosed by this war.

There have been other wars! Wars not inferior in the greatness of the stake, and in the fierce animosity of feelings. During that one which was finished a hundred years ago, it happened that while the English fleet was keeping watch on Brest, an American, perhaps Fulton himself, offered to the maritime Prefect of the port and to the French Admiral, an invention which would sink the unsuspecting English ships one after another—or at any rate, most of them. The offer was not even taken into consideration; and the Prefect ends his report to the Minister of Marine in Paris with a fine phrase of indignation: "It is not the sort of death one would deal to brave men."

And, behold, before history had time to hatch another war of the like proportions in the intensity of aroused passions and the greatness of issues, the dead flavour of archaism descended on the manly sentiment of those self-denying words. Mankind had been demoralised since by its own mastery of mechanical appliances. Its spirit apparently is so weak now, and its flesh has grown so strong, that it will face any deadly horror of destruction and cannot resist the temptation to use any stealthy, murderous contrivance. It has become the intoxicated slave of its own detestable ingenuity. It is true, too, that since the Napoleonic times another sort of war doctrine has been inculcated to a nation, and held out to the world.

IV

On this journey of ours, which for me was essentially not a progress but a retracing of footsteps on a road travelled before, I had no beacons to look out for in Germany. I had never lingered in that land, which, as a whole, is so singularly barren of memorable manifestations of generous sympathies and magnanimous impulses. An ineradicable, invincible provincialism of envy and vanity clings to the forms of its thought like a frowsy garment. Even while yet very young I turned my eyes away from it instinctively, as from a threatening phantom. I believe that children and dogs have, in their innocence, a special power of perception as far as spectral apparitions and coming misfortunes are concerned.

I let myself be carried through Germany as if it were pure space, without sights, without sounds. No whispers of the war reached my voluntary abstraction. And perhaps not so very voluntary, after all! Each of us is a fascinating spectacle to himself, and I had to watch my own personality returning from another world, as it were, to revisit the glimpses of old moons. Considering the condition of humanity, I am, perhaps, not so much to blame for giving myself up to that occupation. We prize the sensation of our continuity, and we can only capture it in that way. By watching.

We arrived in Cracow late at night. After a scrambly supper, I said to my eldest boy, "I can't go to bed. I must go out for a look round. Coming?"

He was ready enough. For him all this was part of the interesting adventure of the whole journey. We stepped out of the portal of the hotel into an empty street, very silent and bright with moonlight. I was indeed revisiting the glimpses of the moon. I felt so much like a ghost that the discovery that I could remember such material things as the right turn to take and the general direction of the street gave me a moment of wistful surprise.

The street, straight and narrow, ran into the great Central Square of the town, the centre of its affairs and of the lighter side of its life. We could see at the far end of the street a promising widening of space. At the corner an unassuming (but armed) policeman, wearing ceremoniously at midnight a pair of white gloves, which made his big hands extremely noticeable, turned his head to look at the grizzled foreigner holding forth in a strange tongue to a youth on whose arm he leaned.

The square, immense in its solitude, was full to the brim of moonlight. The garland of lights at the foot of the houses seemed to burn at the bottom of a bluish pool. I noticed with intimate satisfaction that the unnecessary trees the Municipality persisted in sticking between the stones had been steadily refusing to grow. They were not a bit bigger than the poor victims I could remember. Also, the paving operations seemed to be exactly at the same point at which I left them forty years before. There were the dull, torn-up patches on that lighted expanse, the piles of paving material looking ominously black, like heads of rocks on a silvery sea. Who was it that said Time works wonders? What an exploded superstition! As far as these trees and these paving-stones were concerned it had worked nothing. The suspicion of the unchangeableness of things already vaguely suggested to my senses by our rapid drive from the railway station and by the short walk, was agreeably strengthened within me.

"We are now on the line A.B.," I said to my companion, importantly.

It was the name bestowed in my time to that side of the square by the senior students of that town of classical learning and historical relics. The common citizens knew nothing of it, and even if they had, would not have dreamed of taking it seriously. He who used it was of the initiated, belonged to the Schools. We youngsters regarded that name as a fine jest, the invention of a most excellent fancy. Even as I uttered it to my boy I experienced again that sense of privilege, of initiation. And then, happening to look up at the wall, I saw in the light of the corner lamp, a white, cast-iron tablet fixed thereon, bearing an inscription in raised black letters, thus: "Line A.B." Heavens! The name had been adopted officially! Any town urchin, any guttersnipe, any herb-selling woman of the market-place, any wandering Beotian, was free to talk of the line A.B., to walk on the line A.B., to appoint to meet his friends on the line A.B. It had become a mere name in a directory. I was stunned by the extreme mutability of things. Time *could* work wonders, and no mistake. A Municipality had stolen an invention of excellent fancy, and a fine jest had turned into a horrid piece of cast iron.

I proposed that we should walk to the other end of the line, using the profaned name, not only without gusto, but with positive distaste. And this, too, was one of the wonders of Time, for a bare minute had worked that change. There was at the end of the line a certain street I wanted to look at, I explained to my companion.

To our right the unequal massive towers of St. Mary's Church soared aloft into the ethereal radiance of the air, very black on their shaded sides, glowing with a soft phosphorescent sheen on the others. In the distance the Florian Gate, thick and squat under its pointed roof, barred the street with the square shoulders of the old city wall. In the narrow brilliantly pale vista of bluish flagstones and silvery fronts of houses, its black archway stood out small but very distinct.

There was not a soul in sight, and not even the echo of a footstep for our ears. Into this coldly illuminated and dumb emptiness there issued out of my aroused memory a small boy of eleven, wending his way, not very fast, to a preparatory school for day-pupils on the second floor of the third house down from Florian Gate. It was in the winter months of 1868. At eight o'clock of every morning that God made, sleet or shine, I walked up Florian Street. But of the school I remember very little. I believe that one of my co-sufferers there has become a much appreciated editor of historical documents. But I didn't suffer very much from the various imperfections of my first school. I was rather indifferent to school troubles. I had a private gnawing worm of my own. This was the time of my father's last illness. Every evening at seven, turning my back on the Florian Gate, I walked all the way to a big old house in a quiet little street a good distance beyond the Great Square .There, in a large drawing-room, panelled and bare, with heavy cornices and a lofty ceiling, in a little oasis of light made by two candles in a desert of dusk, I sat at a little table to worry and ink myself all over till the task of preparation was done. The table of my toil faced a tall white double door which was kept closed; but now and then it would come ajar and a nun in a white coif would squeeze herself through, glide across the room and disappear. There were two of these noiseless nursing nuns. Their voices were seldom heard. For indeed what could they have to say! When they did speak to me, it was with their lips hardly moving, in a claustral clear whisper. Domestic matters were ordered by the elderly housekeeper of our neighbour on the second floor, a Canon of the Cathedral, lent for the emergency. She too spoke but seldom. She wore a black dress with a cross hanging by a chain on her ample bosom. And though when she spoke she moved her lips more than the nuns, she never let her voice rise above a peacefully murmuring note. The air around me was all piety, resignation and silence.

I don't know what would have become of me if I had not been a reading boy. My lessons done I would have had nothing to do but sit and watch the awful stillness of the sick-room flow out through the closed white door and coldly enfold my scared heart. I suppose that in a futile childish way I would have gone crazy. But I was a reading boy. There were many books about, lying on consoles, on tables, and even on the floor, for we had not had time to settle down. I read! What did I not read! Sometimes the eldest nun gliding up and casting a mistrustful glance at the open pages would lay her hand lightly on my head and suggest in a doubtful whisper: "Perhaps it isn't very good for you to read these books." I would raise my eyes to her face mutely and with a vague gesture of giving it up she would glide away.

Later in the evening, but not always, I would be permitted to tiptoe into the sick-room to say good-night to the figure prone on the bed which often could not recognise my presence but by a slow movement of the eyes, put my lips dutifully to the nerveless hand lying on the cover-let, and tiptoe out again. Then I would go to bed, in a room at the end of a corridor, and often, not always, cry myself into a good, sound sleep.

I looked forward to what was coming with an incredulous terror. I turned my eyes from it, sometimes with success; and yet all the time I had an awful sensation of the inevitable. I had also moments of revolt which stripped off me some of my simple trust in the government of the universe. But when the inevitable entered the sick-room and the white door was thrown wide open, I don't think I found a single tear to shed. I have a suspicion that the Canon's housekeeper looked upon me as the most callous little wretch on earth.

The day of the funeral came in due course, and all the generous "Youth of the Schools," the grave Senate of the University, the delegations of the trade-guilds, might have obtained (if they cared) *de visu* evidence of the callousness of the little wretch. There was nothing in my aching head but a few words, some such stupid sentences as: "It's done," or "It's accomplished" (in Polish it is much shorter), or something of the sort, repeating itself endlessly. The long procession moved on out of the little street, down a long street, past the Gothic portal of St. Mary's between its unequal towers, towards the Florian Gate.

In the moonlight-flooded silence of the old town of glorious tombs and tragic memories I could see again the small boy of that day following a hearse; a space kept clear in which I walked alone, conscious of an enormous following, the clumsy swaying of the tall black machine, the chanting of the surpliced clergy at the head, the flames of tapers passing under the low archway of the gate, the rows of bared heads on the pavements with fixed, serious eyes. Half the population had turned out on that fine May afternoon. They had not come to honour a great achievement, or even some splendid failure. The dead and they were victims alike of an unrelenting destiny which cut them off from every path of merit and glory. They had come only to render homage to the ardent fidelity of the man whose life had been a fearless confession in word and deed of a creed which the simplest heart in that crowd could feel and understand.

It seemed to me that if I remained longer there in that narrow street I should become the helpless prey of the Shadows I had called up. They were crowding upon me, enigmatic and insistent, in their clinging air of the grave that tasted of dust and in the bitter vanity of all hopes.

"Let's go back to the hotel, my boy," I said. "It's getting late."

It will be easily understood that I neither thought nor dreamt that night of a possible war. For the next two days I went about amongst my fellow men, who welcomed me with the utmost consideration and friendliness, but unanimously derided my fears of a war. They would not believe in it. It was impossible. On the evening of the second day I was in the hotel's smoking-room, an irrationally private apartment, a sanctuary for a few choice minds of the town, always pervaded by a dim religious light, and more hushed than any club reading-room I've ever been in. Gathered into a small knot, we were discussing the situation in subdued tones suitable to the genius of the place.

A gentleman with a fine head of white hair suddenly pointed an impatient finger in my direction and apostrophised me.

"What I want to know is whether, should there be war, England would come in."

The time to draw a breath, and I spoke out for the Cabinet without faltering.

"Most assuredly. I should think all Europe knows that by this time."

He took hold of the lapel of my coat and, giving it a slight jerk for greater emphasis, said forcibly:

"Then if England will, as you say, and all the world knows it, there can be no war. Germany won't be so mad as that."

On the morrow by noon we read of the German ultimatum. The day after came the declaration of war and the Austrian mobilisation order. We were fairly caught. All that remained for me to do was to get my party out of the way of eventual shells. The best move which occurred to me was to snatch them up instantly into the mountains to a Polish health resort of great repute—which I did (at the rate of one hundred miles in eleven hours) by the last civilian train permitted to leave Cracow for the next three weeks.

And there we remained amongst the Poles from all parts of Poland, not officially interned, but simply unable to obtain permission to travel by train or road. It was a wonderful, a poignant two months. This is not the time, and perhaps not the place, to enlarge upon the tragic character of the situation; a whole people seeing the culmination of its misfortunes in a final catastrophe, unable to trust any one, to appeal to any one, to look for help from any quarter; deprived of all hope, and even of its last illusions, and unable in the trouble of minds and the unrest of consciences to take refuge in stoical acceptance. I have seen all this. And I am glad I have not so many years left me to remember that appalling feeling of inexorable Fate, tangible, palpable, come after so many cruel years, a figure of dread, murmuring with iron lips the final words: "Ruin—and Extinction."

But enough of this. For our little band there was the awful anguish of incertitude as to the real nature of events in the West. It is difficult to give an idea how ugly and dangerous things looked to us over there. Belgium knocked down and trampled out of existence, France giving in under repeated blows, a military collapse like that of 1870, and England involved in that disastrous alliance, her army sacrificed, her people in a panic! Polish papers, of course, had no other than German sources of information. Naturally, we did not believe all we heard, but it was sometimes excessively difficult to react with sufficient firmness. We used to shut our door, and there, away from everybody, we sat weighing the news, hunting up discrepancies, scenting lies, finding reasons for hopefulness, and generally cheering each other up. But it was a beastly time. People used to come to me with very serious news and ask, "What do you think of it?" And my invariable answer was, "Whatever has happened or is going to happen, whoever wants to make peace, you may be certain that England will not make it, not for ten years, if necessary."

But enough of this, too. Through the unremitting efforts of Polish friends we obtained at last the permission to travel to Vienna. Once there, the wing of the American Eagle was extended over our uneasy heads. We cannot be sufficiently grateful to the American Ambassador (who all along interested himself in our fate) for his exertions on our behalf, his invaluable assistance, and the real friendliness of his reception in Vienna. Owing to Mr. Penfield's action we obtained permission to leave Austria. And it was a near thing, for his Excellency has informed my American publishers since that a week later orders were issued to have us detained until the end of the war. However, we effected our hair's-breadth escape into Italy and, reaching Genoa, took passage in a Dutch mail-steamer, homeward bound from Java, with London as a port of call.

On that sea route I might have picked up a memory at every mile if the past had not been eclipsed by the tremendous actuality. We saw the signs of it in the emptiness of the Mediterranean, the aspect of Gibraltar, the misty glimpse in the Bay of Biscay of an outward-bound convoy of transports, in the presence of British submarines in the Channel. Innumerable drifters flying the naval flag dotted the narrow waters, and two naval officers coming on board off the South Foreland piloted the ship through the Downs.

The Downs! There they were, thick with the memories of my sea life. But what were to me now the futilities of individual past! As our ship's head swung into the estuary of the Thames a deep, yet faint, concussion passed through the air, a shock rather than a sound, which, missing my ear, found its way straight into my heart. Turning instinctively to look at my boys, I happened to meet my wife's eyes. She also had felt profoundly, coming from far away across the grey distances of the sea, the faint boom of the big guns at work on the coast of Flanders—shaping the future.

JOSEPH CONRAD

LIBERTÀ NELLA VITA

Da un' anno, l' orror della guerra, e l' affanno della coscienza, per comprenderne la inevitabile necessità. L'Antico Libro dice:"*La spada levata per uccidere guarisce talvolta,*" e a nostri giorni, una povera donna del popolo firmo una carta questo affirmando: "*Sia la guerra, per distrugger la guerra;*" e la povera donna del popolo ha due figlioli al fronte.

—Infinita è la strage, e in ogni terra, disperazione e protesta!

—Per tanto dolore nel mondo, per ogni giovane esistenza troncata, sia conquista e diritto, per ogni Patria, il sommo dei beni: La libertà nella Vita.

ELEONORA DUSE

Il Cerro,
  Boscolungo Pistoiese

THE RIGHT TO LIBERTY

[TRANSLATION]

For the past year the horror of war, and the struggle of our minds to comprehend its inevitable necessity!—Holy Writ says:" For all they that take the sword shall perish with the sword," and now in our day a poor woman of the people ends her letter with these words: "There must be war, that war may perish"—and this poor woman of the people has two sons at the front.

Infinite is the suffering, and over the earth wailing and despair!

Through all this sorrow in the world, through all these young lives cut short, may victory bring to every land the crown of life—the right to Liberty.

ELEONORA DUSE

Il Cerro,
  Boscolungo Pistoiese

AUGUSTE RODIN

TWO WOMEN

FROM AN ORIGINAL WATER-COLOUR SKETCH

JOHN GALSWORTHY

HARVEST

THE sky to-night looks as if a million bright angels were passing—a gleaming cloud-mesh drawn across the heaven. One star, very clear, shines beside a full moon white as the globe-campion flower. The wan hills and valleys, the corn-stooks, casting each its shadows, the grey boles of the beeches—all have the remoteness of an ineffable peace. And the past day was so soft, so glamorous; such a hum, such brightness, and the harvest going on. . . .

This last year millions have died with energy but one third spent; millions more unripe for death will yet herald us into the long shades before these shambles cease—boys born just to be the meat of war, spitted on each others' reddened bayonets, without inkling of guilt or knowledge. To what shall we turn that we may keep sane, watching this green, unripe corn, field on field, being scythed by Death for none to eat? There is no solace in the thought: Death is nothing!—save to those who still believe they go straight to Paradise. To us who dare not to know the workings of the Unknowable, and in our heart of hearts cannot tell what, if anything, becomes of us,—to us, the great majority of the modern world—life is valuable, good, a thing worth living out for its natural span. For, if it were not, long ere this we should have sat with folded arms, lifting no hand till the last sighing breath of the human race had whispered itself out into the wind, and a final darkness come; sat, like the Hindu Yogi, watching the sun and moon a little, and expired. The moon would be as white, and the sun as golden if we were gone, the hills and valleys as mysterious, the beech-trees just as they are, only the stooks of corn would vanish with those who garner them. If life were not good we should make of ourselves dust indifferently—we human beings; quietly, peacefully; not in murderous horror reaped by the curving volleys, mown off by rains of shrapnel, and the long yellow scythe of the foul gases. But life is good, and no living thing wishes to die; even they who kill themselves, despairing, resign out of sheer love of life; out of craving for what they have found too mutilated and starved, out of yearning for their meed of joy cruelly frustrated. And they who die that others may live are but those in whom the life-flame burns so hot and bright that they can feel the life and the longing to live in others as if it were their own—more than their own. Yea, life carries with it a very passion for existence.

To what then shall we turn that we may keep sane, watching this harvest of too young deaths, the harvest of the brave, whose stooks are raised before us, casting each its shadow in the ironic moonlight? Green corn! Green corn!

If, having watched those unripe blades reaped off and stacked so pitifully, watched the great dark Waggoner clear those unmellowed fields, we let their sacrifice be vain; if we sow not, hereafter, in a peaceful Earth that which shall become harvest more golden than the world has seen—then Shame on us, unending, in whatever land we dwell. . . .

This harvest night is still. And yet, up there, the bright angels are passing over the moon. One Star!

JOHN GALSWORTHY

August 28, 1915

CLAUDE MONET

BOATS ON A BEACH

FROM AN EARLY CRAYON DRAWING

EDMUND GOSSE

THE ARROGANCE AND SERVILITY OF GERMANY

WE abound, while the war progresses, with examples of the calculated ferocity of the Germans, of their lack of humanity, of their scorn of the generous convention of behaviour. But there is a great danger that on reflection, we may be tempted to regard these developments of savagery as due to the fact of war itself, to a sudden madness of blood-lust, to rage in the face of unanticipated resistance, even to alarm, the emotion of terror being a fruitful source of cruelty as well as of cowardice. It is well, therefore, lest we be tempted to excuse the barbarism of the enemy, to cast our eyes backward and to endeavour to recall what he was in times of peace, in his domestic surroundings, unassailed by anger or fear or ill-humour. I make no apology, then, for recounting an anecdote which illustrates, I think, certain qualities which distinguish the German mentality from that of all the other races which call themselves civilised. The incident which I will proceed to describe was a trifling one, but the impression it left upon my memory was profound.

In the early summer of 1911 my wife and I joined our dear friends, the Dutch novelist Maarten Maartens and his daughter, in a motor-trip through parts of the Rhine Province, and in particular the romantic and volcanic districts of the Eiffel. Maarten Maartens (who died in Holland so lately as the 3rd of August, 1915) was the most delightful travelling companion, and the perfection of his linguistic gifts—for he spoke English, French, Italian and German in each case like a native—made the face of Europe one wide home to him. Our tour was nearly over; we had descended the Moselle, and had paused where the Benedictine Abbey of Laach, on the edge of its serene and wood-encircled crater-lake offers hospitality to the stranger; and then we went down to the Rhine and reached Königswinter late one afternoon. At Königswinter, as travellers know, there is an hotel which Germans brag of as "the best in the world." It is, in fact, or was then, very large, sumptuously furnished, nobly situated on the bastion of the Rhine, looking right over to Drachenfels. The service was rapid and noiseless, the cooking as good as a Teuton kitchen can produce. It had the air of highly-organised prosperity, of a machine exactly suited to harmonise with wealth. To call it " the best hotel in the world" is to show a false conception of excellence as applied to hotels, but it presented everything that German luxury could demand.

We were given a row of excellent rooms on the first floor, with long windows opening on to a terrace which roofed the great restaurant, and whence there was a noble prospect. We went to bed early, and soon the whole vast establishment seemed wrapped in velvet silence. Not a sound broke in the dark warm summer night, not even a whisper from the river. Suddenly an amazing, an unintelligible riot woke the row of us from slumber. The electric light, switched hurriedly on, revealed that the hour was three. In front of us, apparently on our terrace, a turmoil was proceeding of a character to wake the dead. Explosions of glass, what seemed the deeper note of crockery, strange shrieks of metal, bassoon-like and drum-like noises, a deafening roar. Turning off the light, with face pressed to the window, there were dimly to be distinguished phantom-objects descending from above our heads, a shower of vague orbs and bosses, splinters of light, a chaos of the indescribable. Presently the hubbub ceased, deep silence reigned again, and after whispered and bewildered confabulation from door to door, we fell again to dreamless sleep.

In the morning, the riot of the night was our only subject. The terrace in front of our windows showed not the slightest evidence of any disturbance, and we almost doubted our senses. At breakfast, the man who served us knew nothing; he had not wakened all night, he declared. Maarten Maartens, more and more intrigued, insisted on asking the headwaiter. The answer of that worthy was, "There was no disturbance at any time last night. If there had been, I could not have failed to hear it." Maarten Maartens broke from this sturdy liar, and went off to the bureau of the Hotel. Here he found the manager, with whom he was personally acquainted, seated at his desk; two or three other people were near. To the Dutch novelist's inquiry the manager answered—"There was no noise in any part of the hotel at any time last night. You were dreaming,—you had a nightmare." Maarten Maartens, now thoroughly baffled, almost began to think that the noise must have been a delusion of the brain; when the manager, coming to him along a passage, and glancing hither and thither to make sure no one was listening, said, "The officers of a crack regiment from Cologne were supping last night here, in the large private room on the second floor. At three o'clock, as they were leaving, they threw everything that was on the table,—glass, china, silver, everything,—out of window on to the terrace below. But before four o'clock my waiters had removed every trace of what the officers had done. I tell you the facts because you are so persistent, but I must beg you to ask no more questions and make no more remarks. If it were known to the authorities that any complaints had been made, my licence would be withdrawn. My people are so well disciplined, that not a single man or woman employed in the hotel would admit that any incident had taken place." Maarten Maartens said, "But would you allow civilians to behave like that?" "Civilians!" exclaimed the manager; "in their case I should telephone to the police at the crash of the first wineglass."

Before we left Königswinter that day we went with Maarten Maartens to call on the publisher of the German edition of his writings, which had a very large sale. We were received with much ceremony in a modern house, sumptuously furnished, and set in an enchanting park which goes down to the Rhine. The civility of the great publisher and of his family was extreme. In the course of conversation Maarten Maartens, in whom the nocturnal bombardment of his bed-room rankled, told the story with a great deal of humour and liveliness. When he had finished there was a silence, and then the publisher said, very sententiously, "We never criticise the Army! Allow me to show you that part of the garden which has been finished since your last visit!"

This, then, is the spirit in which Germany has arrived at her present amazing development. It renders her unique. Can any one conceive a party of English officers, dining at the Ritz, and hurling all their plates and dishes into the street below? Can any one conceive a party of French civilians, of all classes, accepting a tyranny of arms so humiliating? The arrogance and wantonness of a military aristocracy balanced by an unquestioning servility of the great bulk of the nation. A Kultur of which the watchword is, "We never criticise the Army!" An army in which the qualities of self-respect and respect for others are totally ignored. An amalgam of these contrasted elements makes up the atrocious and formidable temperament of our enemy.

EDMUND GOSSE

MAX BEERBOHM

A GRACIOUS ACT. (CARICATURE)

FROM A WATER-COLOUR SKETCH

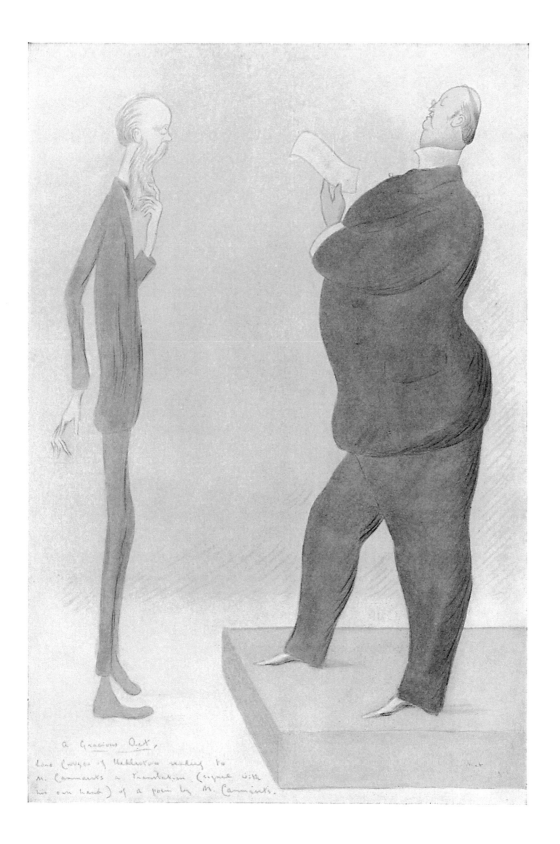

A Gracious Act,

done (course of Mablestone reading to
M. Cammaerts a translation (signed with
his own hand) of a poem by M. Cammaerts.

SCIENCE ET CONSCIENCE

La caractéristique de ce conflit européen sera sans doute, aux yeux de nos descendants, qu'il aura été l'instant où la science aura failli à sa mission. La science, cet attribut des dieux dont l'anoblissement s'est étendu aux mortels depuis le temps de Prométhée, la science, cette conquête pure, cette bienfaitrice, cette aïeule tutélaire, oui! la céleste science, nous l'avons vue, en certaines mains, devenir provisoirement scélérate. Elle a choyé l'incendie, rendu pratiques les milliers d'assassinats par noyade.Elle s'est faite empoisonneuse des poumons, vitrioleuse des visages. Les savants d'outre-Rhin auront passé leurs nuits à chercher quel nouvel attentat aux lois divines et humaines, quel crime inédit pourraient être lancés en défi aux nations, par le mauvais génie de leur science à eux, par cette science qui a réussi à rendre la guerre plus hideuse encore qu'elle n'était de naissance.

' Si c'étaient ces innovations impies qui dussent ouvrir les chemins que prendra l'avenir, alors une guerre future s'emploierait à rendre vénéneux les épis du froment, sophistiquerait les nuages pour que leur ondée verse les épidémies dont les germes sont actuellement découverts ou celles que créerait le travail des laboratoires allemands. La Kultur drainerait les laves des volcans sous les villes, et arrêterait d'avance les étendues d'écorce terrestre à projeter dans l'espace. Et ceux des diverses planètes, qui sont à lorgner la nôtre, constateraient, aux siècles prochains, qu'une monstrueuse science aurait fait de notre Terre, une seconde Lune, sans espèce vivante ni atmosphère, autour de laquelle des satellites soudain mort-nés seraient les continents explosés de l'Ancien-Monde, ou de l'une et l'autre Amériques.

Mais non! Le vieux maître écrivain François Rabelais a écrit: "Science sans conscience est la ruine de l'âme." La science sans conscience sera la ruine aussi des gens qui l'ont choisie pour base de leur empire. La science démoniaque verra briser ses ailes de chauve-souris, par ce pouvoir invisible et impondérable qui, ange gardien des hommes, s'appelle la conscience.

Depuis que la civilisation est en marche, elle va lentement, patiemment, irrésistiblement, vers le mieux, vers le bien. Elle a constitué l'inépuisable réserve, l'invincible armée des valeurs morales, d'où sortent les affranchissements, les justices, les dignités de la race et toute loi de vérité. Cette puissance morale, on a l'Histoire pour en démontrer la constante victoire contre les tyrannies les plus solides, contre les violences les mieux organisées. Mais je n'en veux que la démonstration suivante:

L'État qui a dit que la force prime le droit, l'État qui a piétiné effroyablement toute faiblesse et qui n'a d'égards que pour ce qui est fort, d'où vient que cet État jugea nécessaire de mentir à son peuple, et à la face de tous les peuples sur les vraies causes de la guerre et sur les vrais auteurs responsables? D'où vient que cet État ne manque pas, à chaque occasion, de rééditer le mensonge et de s'y gargariser vainement, ridiculement, follement? Il a marqué ainsi son effroi de la conscience universelle. Celui qui ne s'inquiétait, il y a un an, ni du ciel ni de l'enfer, avait pourtant senti tout de suite, il ne cesse de sentir, aujourd'hui, l'action vengeresse et triomphale s'élaborant dans toutes les consciences de l'humanité, ennemies, neutres, et même sujettes.

PAUL HERVIEU
de l'Académie Française

31 *Juillet* 1915

SCIENCE AND CONSCIENCE

[TRANSLATION]

IT will be left to our descendants to realize that the chief significance of this European conflict lies in its marking the moment when Science failed in her mission. Science, our heritage from the gods, whose high destiny has been fulfilling itself among mortals since the days of Prometheus: Science, mankind's purest conquest, the benefactress, the tutelary guardian—celestial Science, corrupted by strange teachings, has turned and rent us. She has let loose the horror of fire and set her hand to the murder of thousands by drowning. She has poisoned the air that men breathe, and flung vitriol in their faces. Her votaries beyond the Rhine have passed the watches of the night in seeking some new violation of laws human and divine—some undreamt outrage to be launched against the nations by the evil genius of that Science of theirs which has made War, hideous as it was at birth, more loathsome still.

If these unholy innovations were to blaze the way for the future, we should find the war-makers of to-morrow causing the wheat-fields to bear a poisoned harvest and forcing the very clouds in heaven to rain down pestilences whose germs are known to us now, or would in time be brought to birth in the alembics of German laboratories. Kultur would channel the lava of volcanoes under great cities, and hurl into space vast stretches of the earth's crust. The planets of the universe, watching, would learn in centuries to come that a monstrous Science had transformed our World into another Moon, void of life and air, around which swim still-born satellites that were once the blasted continents of the Old World or the Americas.

But this is not to be. The old master-writer, François Rabelais, has said: "Science without conscience spells ruin to the soul." And so Science without conscience must mean the destruction of that nation which has chosen it as the foundation of empire. Demoniacal Science, dragon-winged, will be shattered against that invisible and imponderable force, the guardian angel of mankind, which is called Conscience.

From the dawn of civilization it has moved slowly, patiently, irresistibly toward the better, toward the good. It has constituted the inexhaustible reserve, the invincible army of moral values, out of which the liberties, the justices, the dignities of the race, and every law of truth, have come to being. History stands ready to number the victories of this moral force over the most strongly organized lawlessness and the mightiest tyrannies. And I ask no better demonstration than this:

The State which has declared that might is right, which has trampled under foot all weakness and respects only that which is strong—how comes it that this State finds itself constrained to lie to its own people and to all the nations about the true causes of this war and the men who are responsible for it? How comes it that this State never fails, whenever chance offers, to repeat the dreary lie and mouth it over desperately, absurdly, vainly? Thus does it betray its terror of the universal Conscience. The power which, one year ago, feared neither heaven nor hell, felt instantly and must ever feel the avenging and triumphant assault of all the consciences of humanity—enemy, neutral, and even subject to itself.

PAUL HERVIEU
de l'Académie Française

July 31, 1915

J. L. GÉRÔME

TURKISH SOLDIER

FROM THE ORIGINAL PENCIL DRAWING MADE IN 1857

Avamate —
J. youth (haute - Egypte) —

JL Gérôme
1857

GÉNÉRAL HUMBERT

LES ARABES AVAIENT RAISON

LE 28 août 1914, après une sanglante bataille, la Ière Division du Maroc avait refoulé l'ennemi de la Fosse à l'Eau dans la direction de Thin-le-Moutiers.

La nuit venue, malgré des pertes cruelles, la satisfaction était grande: chacun espérait pour le lendemain l'achèvement de la victoire.

Mais contrairement à ces prévisions, l'ordre arriva, sur le coup de onze heures du soir, de se dégager au plus vite et de marcher en retraite vers les plateaux qui dominent à l'Est la route de Mézières à Rethel.

Ce mouvement était une conséquence de la manœuvre géniale conçue dès le 25 août par le Général JOFFRE et qui devait aboutir, comme chacun sait, à la victoire de la Marne; mais nous l'ignorions.

Donc, il fallut se "décrocher" immédiatement. La nuit était très noire; les troupes accablées par une dure journée de combat, couchaient sur leurs positions.

Néanmoins, les ordres se transmirent rapidement et, à minuit, dans un silence complet, la Division retraitait en plusieurs colonnes face à l'Est.

L'ennemi allait-il éventer le mouvement? Il faillait craindre en tout cas qu'à l'aube, c'est à dire après 3 heures de marche, il ne s'en aperçut et ne commençat une poursuite qui aurait été fort gênante.

Il nous aurait en effet rattrapés au pied du plateau, alors que la Division était obligée de se former en une colonne de route unique pour y accéder.

Mais, contrairement à nos craintes rien ne gêna notre opération; à midi, les troupes étaient rassemblées et en ordre parfait dans les environs de Neuvizy, à l'Est de Launois.

Que s'était-il passé? L'ennemi était-il resté sur place? Avait-il lui-même battu en retraite?

C'est dans la journée seulement que l'explication de son attitude nous fut connue.

Par suite de l'obscurité de la nuit ou pour tout autre motif, un bataillon de Tirailleurs Algériens, celui du Commandant Mignerot, n'avait pas été touché par l'ordre de repliement.

Il était en toute première ligne et ne possédait d'autre ordre que celui qu'il avait reçu la veille en fin de journée: "Avant-postes de combat; résister à tout prix."

Aussi à l'aube, lorsque l'ennemi se rendant compte enfin de notre dérobade, voulut pousser de l'avant, il trouva, au centre de notre front, tel qu'il était la veille, ce bataillon en position, ferme, résolu à exécuter son ordre coûte que coûte.

La lutte, au dire des témoins, fut homérique; accablé par des forces supérieures, écrasé par l'artillerie, le bataillon résista sur place d'abord, puis lorsqu'il fut enveloppé sur ses ailes, recula pas à pas, défendant vigoureusement chaque pouce de terrain.

C'est cette superbe attitude qui, à mon insu, assura à la Division, le temps voulu pour exécuter son ascension sur le plateau.

Mais, hélas, ce fut au prix des plus douloureux sacrifices; ce magnifique bataillon qui comptait plus de 1,000 combattants avait perdu le Commandant, la plupart des officiers et 600 hommes.

Au cours de cette glorieuse résistance se produisit l'incident que je veux raconter.

Lorsque le repli commença, il ne pouvait être question de relever morts ou blessés.—Grande fut la stupéfaction des Arabes. C'étaient de vieux soldats, qui avaient combattu un peu partout, en Algérie, au Maroc; toujours ils avaient vu leurs chefs veiller soigneusement à ce qu'aucun blessé, aucun cadavre ne risquât d'être massacré ou profané par l'ennemi—le Berbère ou le Chleuh.—Voici que cette fois, on abandonnait les blessés et les morts. Ils n'en croyaient pas leurs yeux. Des murmures s'élevèrent dans les rangs; un vieux sergent alla même jusqu'à menacer de son fusil un officier en l'appelant traître.

On eut toutes les peines du monde à leur rappeler ce qu'on leur avait pourtant dit: dans les armées de l'Europe, les blessés, les morts, lorsqu'ils tombent aux mains de l'ennemi constituent un dépôt sacré ; ils sont traités avec humanité, avec respect.

Hélas, les Arabes avaient raison. Combien de fois l'avons-nous constaté avec indignation et colère !

Mais, au début de la guerre, qui de nous n'eût pas accordé à l'ennemi les sentiments qui sont l'honneur d'une armée : la générosité, l'humanité, le respect des conventions, de la parole donné ?

Qui eut imaginé que 45 ans de " Kultur " produiraient de si tristes résultats ?

Heureusement, nous avons trouvé à ces désillusions de douces consolations :

Comme tout se compense dans l'univers, il s'est rencontré des âmes exquises qui se sont ingéniées à opposer aux misères de la guerre, les remèdes les plus touchants.

Telle est l'œuvre des Sans-Foyer.

Pour les bienfaits qu'elle a prodigués, pour les nombreux affligés qu'elle a secourus, notre reconnaissance lui est acquise.

Honneur à ses Fondateurs.

GÉNÉRAL HUMBERT

Q. G. IIIe Armée, 28 *Août* 1915

AN HEROIC STAND

[TRANSLATION]

On the 28th of August, 1914, after a hard-fought battle, the First Moroccan Division drove the enemy back from la Fosse à l'Eau, in the direction of Thin-le-Moutiers.

Despite our many losses we were exultant when night fell, and confident of winning a decisive victory the next morning.

But at eleven o'clock, contrary to our expectations, we got an order to retreat at once towards the east, in the direction of the heights which command the road from Mézières to Rethel.

This movement was part of the strategic plan made by General Joffre on the 25th of August, a plan which led, as every one now knows, to the victory of the Marne—but of that we knew nothing at the time.

The night was pitch dark. The men, worn out by the long day's fighting, had fallen asleep where they had halted, but the order was rapidly transmitted, and at midnight, in dead silence, the columns of our Division set their faces eastward.

There was a chance that the enemy might discover our purpose. We feared that in three hours when daylight came, we should be pursued, and if we were overtaken it might be awkward, for, to mount to the plateau that lay ahead of us the Division would be obliged to take the narrow road in single column.

Nothing, however, interfered with us; we carried our movement through successfully, and soon the troops were assembled in perfect order to the east of Launois, near Neuvizy.

We could not understand why we had not been molested. Had the enemy remained where we left him, or had he retreated?

Later in the day we learnt the reason of our security. Because of the darkness, or for some other reason, the order to fall back was not transmitted to a battalion of the Tirailleurs Algériens, led by Commandant Mignerot.

The battalion therefore remained where it was, in the first fighting line, in obedience to an order of the day before, which had been to hold its ground at whatever cost.

Thus at dawn, when the enemy found we had given him the slip, and tried to follow us up, this battalion, bent on carrying out the only order it had received, was there to face him.

Those who saw the battle said it was Homeric. Overwhelmed by superior numbers, crushed by artillery, the battalion at first fought where it stood, and then, enveloped on both wings, fell back step by step, fiercely contesting every inch of ground.

GENERAL HUMBERT

That splendid stand gave the Division time to climb the heights in safety. But a heavy price was paid; when the fight began the battalion numbered more than a thousand; when it was over the Commandant, almost all his officers and six hundred of his men were dead.

It was in the course of this glorious resistance that the following incident took place. When the battalion was forced back it was impossible to carry off the dead and wounded. The Arabs were amazed. They were old soldiers who had fought all over Morocco and Algeria, and they had always seen their leaders take the utmost care that no wounded comrades, no corpse of a brave man, should be left behind to be massacred or defiled by savage tribesmen. And now they were abandoning their wounded and their dead. They could not believe their eyes; murmurs arose from the ranks; one old sergeant went so far as to menace his officer with his rifle and call him "traitor."

Often as they had been told by their chiefs of the respect with which the dead and wounded are treated by European armies, it was almost impossible to reassure them as to the fate of their comrades.

How often since, alas, with bitter wrath, we have had reason to recall their instinctive distrust of the foe!

But in those early days of the war, which one of us would have hesitated to give our enemies credit for the feelings which are part of an Army's very soul: generosity, humanity, respect for the word of honour?

Who could have imagined that forty-five years of "Kultur" would have borne such fruit?

Fortunately there is consolation even for such disillusionment. This is a universe of compensations, and compassionate souls are striving to lessen the inevitable misery of this most terrible of wars.

Among them we gladly reckon those who come to the aid of the Homeless. And in the name of the many helpless sufferers whom they relieve we offer them our gratitude.

GENERAL HUMBERT
Commanding the Third Army of France

JOHN SINGER SARGENT, R.A.

PORTRAIT OF HENRY JAMES

FROM A PHOTOGRAPH OF THE ORIGINAL PAINTING

THE LONG WARDS

Tʜᴇʀᴇ comes back to me out of the distant past an impression of the citizen soldier at once in his collective grouping and in his impaired, his more or less war-worn state, which was to serve me for long years as the most intimate vision of him that my span of life was likely to disclose. This was a limited affair indeed, I recognise as I try to recover it, but I mention it because I was to find at the end of time that I had kept it in reserve, left it lurking deep down in my sense of things, however shyly and dimly, however confusedly even, as a term of comparison, a glimpse of something by the loss of which I should have been the poorer; such a residuary possession of the spirit, in fine, as only needed darkness to close round it a little from without in order to give forth a vague phosphorescent light. It was early, it must have been very early, in our Civil War, yet not so early but that a large number of those who had answered President Lincoln's first call for an army had had time to put in their short period (the first term was so short then, as was likewise the first number,) and reappear again in camp, one of those of their small New England State, under what seemed to me at the hour, that of a splendid autumn afternoon, the thickest mantle of heroic history. If I speak of the impression as confused I certainly justify that mark of it by my failure to be clear at this moment as to how much they were in general the worse for wear—since they can't have been exhibited to me, through their waterside settlement of tents and improvised shanties, in anything like hospital conditions. However, I cherish the rich ambiguity, and have always cherished it, for the sake alone of the general note exhaled, the thing that has most kept remembrance unbroken. I carried away from the place *the* impression, the one that not only was never to fade, but was to show itself susceptible of extraordinary eventual enrichment. I may not pretend now to refer it to the more particular sources it drew upon at that summer's end of 1861, or to say why my repatriated warriors were, if not somehow definitely stricken, so largely either lying in apparent helplessness or moving about in confessed languor: it suffices me that I have always thought of them as expressing themselves at almost every point in the minor key, and that this has been the reason of their interest. What I call the note therefore is the characteristic the most of the essence and the most inspiring—inspiring I mean for consideration of the admirable sincerity that we thus catch in the act: the note of the quite abysmal softness, the exemplary genius for accommodation, that forms the alternative aspect, the passive as distinguished from the active, of the fighting man whose business is in the first instance formidably to bristle. This aspect has been produced, I of course recognise, amid the horrors that the German powers had, up to a twelvemonth ago, been for years conspiring to let loose upon the world by such appalling engines and agencies as mankind had never before dreamed of; but just that is the lively interest of the fact unfolded to us now on a scale beside which, and though save indeed for a single restriction, the whole previous illustration of history turns pale. Even if I catch but in a generalising blur that exhibition of the first American levies as a measure of experience had stamped and harrowed them, the signally attaching mark that I refer to is what I most recall; so that if I didn't fear, for the connection, to appear to compare the slighter things with the so much greater, the diminished shadow with the far-spread substance, I should speak of my small old scrap of truth, miserably small in contrast with the immense evidence even then to have been gathered, but in respect to which latter occasion didn't come to me, as having contained possibilities of development that I must have languished well-nigh during a lifetime to crown it with.

One had during the long interval not lacked opportunity for a vision of the soldier at peace, moving to and fro with a professional eye on the horizon, but not fished out of the bloody welter and laid down to pant, as we actually see him among the Allies, almost on the very bank and within sound and sight of his deepest element. The effect of many of the elapsing years, the time in England and France and Italy, had indeed been to work his collective presence so closely and familiarly into any human scene pretending to a full illustration of our most generally approved conditions that I confess to having missed him rather distressfully from the picture of things offered me during a series of months spent not long ago in a few American cities after years of disconnection. I can scarce say why I missed him sadly rather than gladly—I might so easily have prefigured one's delight in his absence; but certain it is that my almost outraged consciousness of our practically doing without him amid American conditions was a revelation of the degree in which his great imaging, his great reminding and enhancing function is rooted in the European basis. I felt his non-existence on the American positively produce a void which nothing else, as a vivifying substitute, hurried forward to fill; this being indeed the case with many of the other voids, the most aching, which left the habituated eye to cast about as for something to nibble in a state of dearth. We never know, I think, how much these wanting elements have to suggest to the pampered mind till we feel it living in view of the community from which they have been simplified away. On these occasions they conspire with the effect of certain other, certain similar expressions, examples of social life proceeding as by the serene, the possibly too serene, process of mere ignorance, to bring to a head for the fond observer the wonder of what is supposed to strike, for the projection of a furnished world, the note that they are not there to strike. However, as I quite grant the hypothesis of an observer still fond and yet remarking the lapse of the purple patch of militarism but with a joy unclouded, I limit myself to the merely personal point that the fancy of a particular brooding analyst *could* so sharply suffer from a vagueness of privation, something like an unseasoned observational diet, and then, rather to his relief, find the mystery cleared up. And the strict relevancy of the bewilderment I glance at, moreover, becomes questionable, further, by reason of my having, with the outbreak of the horrors in which we are actually steeped, caught myself staring at the exhibited militarism of the general British scene not much less ruefully than I could remember to have stared, a little before, at the utter American deficit. Which proves after all that the rigour of the case had begun at a bound to defy the largest luxury of thought; so that the presence of the military in the picture on the mere moderate insular scale struck one as "furnishing" a menaced order but in a pitiful and pathetic degree.

The degree was to alter, however, by swift shades, just as one's comprehension of the change grew and grew with it; and thus it was that, to cut short the record of our steps and stages, we have left immeasurably behind us here the question of what might or what should have been. That belonged, with whatever beguiled or amused ways of looking at it, to the abyss of our past delusion, a collective state of mind in which it had literally been possible to certain sophists to argue that, so far from not having soldiers enough, we had more than we were likely to know any respectable public call for. It was in the very fewest weeks that we replaced a pettifogging consciousness by the most splendidly liberal, and, having swept through all the first phases of anxiety and suspense, found no small part of our measure of the matter settle down to an almost luxurious study of our multiplied defenders after the fact, as I may call it, or in the light of that acquaintance with them as products supremely tried and tested which I began by speaking of. We were up to our necks in this relation before we could turn round, and what upwards of a year's experience of it has done in the contributive and enriching way may now well be imagined. I might feel that my marked generalisation, the main hospital impression, steeps the case in too strong or too stupid a synthesis, were it not that to consult my memory, a recollection of countless associative contacts, is to see the emphasis almost absurdly thrown on my quasi-paradox. Just so it is of singular interest for the witnessing mind itself to feel the happy truth stoutly resist any qualifying hint—since I *am* so struck with the charm, as I can only call it, of the tone and temper of the man of action, the creature appointed to advance and explode and destroy, and elaborately instructed as to how to do these things, reduced to helplessness in the innumerable instances now surrounding us. It does n't in the least take the edge from my impression that his sweet reasonableness, representing the opposite end of his wondrous scale, is probably the very oldest story of the touching kind in the world; so far indeed from my claiming the least originality for the appealing appearance as it has lately reached me from so many sides, I find its suggestion of vast communities, communities of patience and placidity, acceptance submission pushed to the last point, to be just what makes the whole show most illuminating.

"Wonderful that, from east to west, they must *all* be like this," one says to one's self in presence of certain consistencies, certain positive monotonies of aspect; "wonderful that if joy of battle (for the classic term, in spite of new horrors, seems clearly still to keep its old sense,) has, to so attested a pitch, animated these forms, the disconnection of spirit should be so prompt and complete, should hand the creature over as by the easiest turn to the last refinements of accommodation. The disconnection of the flesh, of physical function in whatever ravaged area, *that* may well be measureless; but how interesting, if the futility of such praise doesn't too much dishonour the subject, the exquisite anomaly of the intimate readjustment of the really more inflamed and exasperated part, or in other words of the imagination, the captured, the haunted vision, to life at its most innocent and most ordered!" To that point one's unvarying thought of the matter; which yet, though but a meditation without a conclusion, becomes the very air in which fond attention spends itself. So far as commerce of the acceptable, the tentatively helpful kind goes, one looks for the key to success then, among the victims, exactly on that ground of the apprehension pacified and almost, so to call it, trivialised. The attaching thing becomes thus one's intercourse with the imagination of the particular patient subject, the individual himself, in the measure in which this interest bears us up and carries us along; which name for the life of his spirit has to cover, by a considerable stretch, all the ground. By the stretch of the name, moreover, I am far from meaning any stretch of the faculty itself—which remains for the most part a considerably contracted or inert force, a force in fact often so undeveloped as to be insusceptible of measurement at all, so that one has to resort, in face of the happy fact that communion still does hold good, to some other descriptive sign for it. That sign, however, fortunately presents itself with inordinate promptitude and fits to its innocent head with the last perfection the cap, in fact the very crown, of an office that we can only appraise as predetermined goodnature. We after this fashion score our very highest on behalf of a conclusion, I think, in feeling that whether or no the British warrior's goodnature has much range of fancy, his imagination, whatever there may be of it, is at least so goodnatured as to show absolutely everything it touches, everything without exception, even the worst machinations of the enemy, in that colour. Variety and diversity of exhibition, in a world virtually divided as now into hospitals and the preparation of subjects for them, are, I accordingly conceive, to be looked for quite away from the question of physical patience, of the general consent to suffering and mutilation, and, instead of that, in this connection of the sort of mind and thought, the sort of moral attitude, that are born of the sufferer's other relations; which I like to think of as being different from country to country, from class to class, and as having their fullest national and circumstantial play.

It would be of the essence of these remarks, could I give them within my space all the particular applications naturally awaiting them, that they pretend to refer here to the British private soldier only—generalisation about his officers would take us so considerably further and so much enlarge our view. The high average of the beauty and modesty of these, in the stricken state, causes them to affect me, I frankly confess, as probably the very flower of the human race. One's apprehension of "Tommy" —and I scarce know whether more to dislike the liberty this mode of reference takes with him, or to incline to retain it for the tenderness really latent in it—is in itself a theme for fine notation, but it has brought me thus only to the door of the boundless hospital ward in which, these many months, I have seen the successive and the so strangely quiet tides of his presence ebb and flow, and it stays me there before the incalculable vista. The perspective stretches away, in its mild order, after the fashion of a tunnel boring into the very character of the people, and so going on forever—never arriving or coming out, that is, at anything in the nature of a station, a junction or a terminus. So it draws off through the infinite of the common personal life, but planted and bordered, all along its passage, with the thick-growing flower of the individual illustration, this sometimes vivid enough and sometimes pathetically pale. The great fact, to my now so informed vision, is that it undiscourageably continues and that an unceasing repetition of its testifying particulars seems never either to exhaust its sense or to satisfy that of the beholder. Its sense indeed, if I may so far simplify, is pretty well always the same, that of the jolly fatalism above-mentioned, a state of moral hospitality to the practices of fortune, however outrageous, that may at times fairly be felt as providing amusement, providing a new and thereby a refreshing turn of the personal situation, for the most interested party. It is true that one may be sometimes moved to wonder which *is* the most interested party, the stricken subject in his numbered bed or the friendly, the unsated inquirer who has tried to forearm himself against such a measure of the " criticism of life" as might well be expected to break upon him from the couch in question, and who yet, a thousand occasions for it having been, all round him, inevitably neglected, finds this ingenious provision quite left on his hands. He may well ask himself what he is to do with people who so consistently and so comfortably content themselves with *being*—being for the most part incuriously and instinctively admirable—that nothing whatever is left of them for reflection as distinguished from their own practice; but the only answer that comes is the reproduction of the note. He may, in the interest of appreciation, try the experiment of lending them some scrap of a complaint or a curse in order that they shall meet him on congruous ground, the ground of encouragement to his own participating impulse. They are imaged, under that possibility, after the manner of those unfortunates, the very poor, the victims of a fire or shipwreck, to whom you have to lend something to wear before they can come to thank you for helping them. The inmates of the long wards, however, have no use for any imputed or derivative sentiments or reasons; they feel in their own way, they feel a great deal, they don't at all conceal from you that to have seen what they have seen is to have seen things horrible and monstrous—but there is no estimate of them for which they seek to be indebted to you, and nothing they less invite from you than to show them that such visions must have poisoned their world. Their world is n't in the least poisoned: they have assimilated their experience by a process scarce at all to be distinguished from their having healthily got rid of it.

The case thus becomes for you that they consist wholly of their applied virtue, which is accompanied with no waste of consciousness whatever. The virtue may strike you as having been, and as still being, greater in some examples than others, but it has throughout the same sign of differing at almost no point from a supreme amiability. How can creatures so amiable, you allow yourself vaguely to wonder, have welcomed even for five minutes the stress of carnage? and how can the stress of carnage, the murderous impulse at the highest pitch, have left so little distortion of the moral nature? It has left none at all that one has at the end of many months been able to discover; so that perhaps the most steadying and refreshing effect of intercourse with these hospital friends is through the almost complete rest from the facing of generalisations to which it treats you. One would even like perhaps, as a stimulus to talk, more generalisation; but one gets enough of that out in the world, and one does n't get there nearly so much of what one gets in this perspective, the particular perfect sufficiency of the extraordinary principle, whatever it is, which makes the practical answer so supersede any question or any argument that it seems fairly to have acted by chronic instinctive anticipation, the habit of freely throwing the personal weight into any obvious opening. The personal weight, in its various forms and degrees, is what lies there with a head on the pillow and whatever wise bandages there-

about or elsewhere, and it becomes interesting in itself, and just in pro-
portion, I think, to its having had all its history after the fact. All its
history is that of the particular application which has brought it to the
pass at which you find it, and is a stream roundabout which you have to
press a little hard to make it flow clear. Then, in many a case, it does
flow, certainly, as clear as one could wish, and with the strain that it is
always somehow English history and illustrates afresh the English way
of doing things and regarding them, of feeling and naming them. The
sketch extracted is apt to be least coloured when the prostrate historian,
as I may call him, is an Englishman of the English; it has more point,
though not perhaps more essential tone, when he is a Scot of the Scots,
and has most when he is an Irishman of the Irish; but there is absolutely
no difference, in the light of race and save as by inevitable variation from
individual to individual, about the really constant and precious matter,
the attested possession on the part of the contributor of a free loose un-
disciplined quantity of being to contribute.

This is the palpable and ponderable, the admirably appreciable, re-
siduum — as to which if I be asked just how it is that I pluck the flower
of amiability from the bramble of an individualism so bristling with accents, I am afraid I can only say that the accents would seem by the
mercy of chance to fall together in the very sense that permits us to de-
tach the rose with the fewest scratches. The rose of active goodnature,
irreducible, incurable, or in other words all irreflective, *that* is the variety which the individualistic tradition happens, up and down these islands,
to wear upon its ample breast — even it may be with a considerable effect
of monotony. There it is, for what it is, and the very simplest summary
of one's poor bedside practice is perhaps to confess that one has most of
all kept one's nose buried in it. There hangs about the poor practitioner
by that fact, I profess, an aroma not doubtless at all mixed or in the least
mystical, but so unpervertedly wholesome that what can I pronounce it
with any sort of conscience but sweet? That is the rough, unless I rather
say the smooth, report of it; which covers of course, I hasten to add, a

constant shift of impression within the happy limits. Did I not, by way of introduction to these awaiters of articulate acknowledgment, find myself first of all, early in the autumn, in presence of the first aligned rows of lacerated Belgians?—the eloquence of whose mere mute expression of their state, and thereby of their cause, remains to me a vision unforgettable forever, and this even though I may not here stretch my scale to make them, Flemings of Flanders though they were, fit into my remarks with the English of the English and the Scotch of the Scotch. If other witnesses might indeed here fit in they would decidedly come nearest, for there were aspects under which one might almost have taken them simply for Britons comparatively starved of sport and, to make up for that, on straighter and homelier terms with their other senses and appetites. But their effect, thanks to their being so seated in everything that their ripe and rounded temperament had done for them, was to make their English entertainers, and their successors in the long wards especially, seem ever so much more complicated—besides making of what had happened to themselves, for that matter, an enormity of outrage beyond all thought and all pity. Their fate had cut into their spirit to a peculiar degree through their flesh, as if they had had an unusual thickness of this, so to speak—which up to that time had protected while it now but the more exposed and, collectively, entrapped them; so that the ravaged and plundered domesticity that one felt in them, which was mainly what they had to oppose, made the terms of their exile and their suffering an extension of the possible and the dreadful. But all that vision is a chapter by itself—the essence of which is perhaps that it has been the privilege of this placid and sturdy people to show the world a new shade and measure of the tragic and the horrific. The first wash of the great Flemish tide ebbed at any rate from the hospitals—creating moreover the vast needs that were to be so unprecedentedly met, and the native procession which has prompted these remarks set steadily in. I have played too uncertain a light, I am well aware, not arresting it at half the possible points, yet with one aspect of the case staring out so straight as to form the vivid moral that asks to be drawn. The deepest impression from the sore human stuff with which such observation deals is that of its being strong and sound in an extraordinary degree for the conditions producing it. These conditions represent, one feels at the best, the crude and the waste, the ignored and neglected state; and under the sense of the small care and scant provision that have attended such hearty and happy growths, struggling into life and air with no furtherance to speak of, the question comes pressingly home of what a better economy might, or verily might n't, result in. If this abundance all slighted and unencouraged can still comfort us, what would n't it do for us tended and fostered and cultivated? That is my moral, for I believe in Culture—speaking strictly now of the honest and of our own congruous kind.

HENRY JAMES

LÉON BAKST

MÉNADE

FROM A WATER-COLOUR SKETCH

MÉNADE

BAKST
1915

MAURICE MAETERLINCK

NOTRE HÉRITAGE

Sı l'on pouvait suivre des yeux ce qui se passe dans le monde idéal qui nous domine de toutes parts, on constaterait sans nul doute que rien ne se perd sur les champs de bataille. Ce que nos admirables morts abandonnent, c'est à nous qu'ils le lèguent; et quand ils périssent pour nous, ce n'est pas métaphoriquement et d'une manière détournée, mais très réellement et d'une façon directe qu'ils nous laissent leur vie. Tout homme qui succombe dans un acte de gloire émet une vertu qui redescend sur nous, et dans la violence d'une fin prématurée, rien ne s'égare et rien ne s'évapore. Il donne en grand et d'un seul coup ce qu'il eût donné dans une longue existence de devoir et d'amour. La mort n'entame pas la vie; elle ne peut rien contre elle. Le total de celle-ci demeure toujours pareil. Ce qu'elle enlève à ceux qui tombent passe en ceux qui restent debout. La mort ne gagne rien tant qu'il y a des vivants. Plus elle exerce ses ravages, plus elle augmente l'intensité de ce qu'elle n'atteint point; plus elle poursuit ses victoires illusoires, mieux elle nous prouve que l'humanité finira par la vaincre.

MAURICE MAETERLINCK

OUR INHERITANCE

[TRANSLATION]

IF our vision could open on that unseen world which dominates us from all sides, we should unquestionably learn that on the battlefields there can be no loss. The heritage which our splendid soldiers yield up in dying is bequeathed to us; and when they perish for our sakes, they give us their lives in no metaphoric, roundabout sense, but really and directly. From every man who meets death gloriously there goes forth a virtue which enters into us, and even in the violence of an untimely end nothing goes astray or vanishes. In one short moment the soldier gives open-handed the offering of an entire lifetime of love and duty. Death is power-less to prevail over Life. Its total remains forever unchanged. That which is taken from the fallen passes on to those left standing. While men still live, Death can win nothing. The more desperate its efforts, the brighter burns the flame it would fain extinguish; the more cruelly it pursues its phantom victories, the clearer is it proven that in the end Humanity must surely vanquish.

Maurice Maeterlinck

Translated by J. G. D. Paul

EDWARD SANDFORD MARTIN

WE WHO SIT AFAR OFF

"I, skeptic though I am, am, like every Englishman, a mystic. I see in this war almost literally a fight between God and the Devil. . . . With all my soul I believe that the ideal of pity is the noblest thing we have, and that its denial which waves on every German flag is the denial of all that the greatest men have striven for for centuries. . . . I feel that the two enormous spirits that move this world are showing their weapons almost visibly, and that never was the garment of the living world so thin over the gods that it conceals.

"I am not much elated by the thought. I have little opinion of Providence as an ally, and I am surprised at the weakness the Kaiser shows for his pocket deity. What we have to do, in my opinion, we do ourselves, and our task is none the lighter that we defend the right. But I am hardened and set by the thing I believe. We feel that we are fighting for the life of England—yes, for the safety of France—yes, for the sanctity of treaties—yes, but behind these secondary and comparatively material issues, for something far deeper, far greater, for something so great and deep that if our efforts fail I pray God I may die before I see it."

These are words from a letter of an English physician with the British expeditionary force to an American physician who had sent him Dr. Eliot's war-book. He, in the war, disclosing how he feels about it, has described also how it seems to thousands of us who are looking on. We too are mystics in our feelings about this war. We too have, and have had almost from the first, this profound sense of a fundamental conflict between the powers of good and evil, the soul of the world at grips with its body.

And while we feel so profoundly that the Allies are on the Lord's side, a good many of us at least prefer the English doctor's small reliance on Providence as an ally to the Kaiser's proprietary confidence in the Almighty's backing. It is not safe to count on Providence to win for us.

He knows us much better than we know ourselves, and may have views for our improvement and the world's which our minds do not fathom and which do not match our plans. Nevertheless, in a vast crisis to feel one's self on the Lord's side, there to fight, win or lose, there to stay, alive or dead, is an enormous stay to the spirit. "I am hardened and set," says the English doctor, "by the thing I believe." Then truly is Providence his ally.

To work is to pray; to fight is to pray; to tend the wounded in hospitals and avert disease is to pray. The people in action are quickened and sustained in their faith by their exertions, but what of us who sit afar off in safety and look on at Armageddon?

Our case is pretty trying. When the war first came it was hard for the thousands of us who cared, to sleep in our beds. We felt it was our war, too, and it was, for we too are Europeans, and have besides as great a stake in civilization as any one has. We have kept up our habit of sleeping in our beds because that was more convenient and there was no advantage to any one in our doing otherwise. And we have gone on without much outward change in our work and our habits of life. And we have grown a little callous, and doubtless a little torpid, and lost some of the ardor that came with the first shock. Nevertheless, hundreds of thousands of Americans have had one continuing, underlying thought for a year and a quarter—the war, the great conflict between good and evil, and what to do about it.

There never has been a moment's doubt about which side would be ours if we went in. But how get in? Where lies duty? By what course may we best help? Is it our war? When and how will the mandate come to us, too, to resist the crushing of civilization under the Prussian jackboot? There are millions of Americans who want to get into the war, but there are more millions who want to keep out. Our English doctor appreciates the predicament of neutral countries, and this is what he says about it:

"War being what it is, it is hopeless to expect that any nation will engage in it who does not fear great loss or hope great gain. Nations will always be swayed by the influences which are now swaying Italy, Greece, Bulgaria and Rumania. No desire of justice would lead those countries to join us. I doubt if it would justify their rulers in declaring war."

Perhaps that is another way of saying that no country will get into the war that dares to stay out. Nations, especially democratic nations, are not much like men. They may not say, "I will fight for you; I will spend my strength and treasure for you; I will die for you and your cause." Individuals may feel, say, do all that, but individuals are not nations. A nation says: "The laws of my being must determine my conduct. I must go my own gait according to those rules. But if war stretches across my path I need not turn out for it."

How far this war has still to go, no one knows. It may still, any day, stretch across the path of the United States, so that the natural drive of our procedure will carry us into it.

EDWARD SANDFORD MARTIN

JOHN SINGER SARGENT, R.A.

TWO HEADS

FROM A PENCIL DRAWING

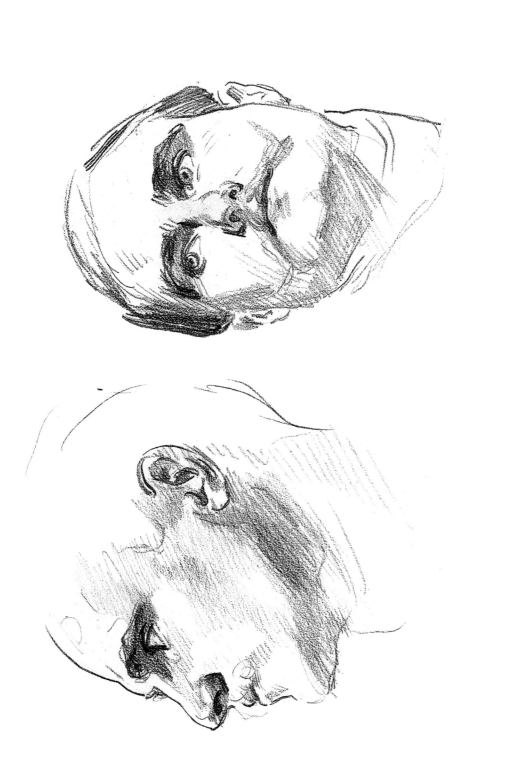

PAUL ELMER MORE

A MOMENT OF TRAGIC PURGATION

LET me say forthwith that this is a book which I shall read with deep interest, but to which I contribute reluctantly. There is gloom enough in the air, and I see no profit in adding the scruples and doubts of my troubled mind to the general sum. For I can find little reason for hope in the evils that have fallen upon the world; and where are the signs of the wisdom that is to be born of these calamitous times? When all is over and in the hush of desolation we have leisure to reckon up the cost of our madness, will it appear that we have learned the meaning of the sentimental shirking of realities? Or shall we continue, as we have done for a century and more, to place sympathy above justice, and to forget the responsibility of the individual in our insistence on the obligations of society; inflaming the passions of men by rebellious outcries against the unequal dealings of Fate, relaxing the immediate bonds of duty by vague dreams of the brotherhood of man, weakening character by reluctance to pursue crime with punishment, preparing the way for outbursts of hatred by fostering the emotions at the expense of reason; and then, in alarm at our effeminacy, rushing to the opposite glorification of sheer force and efficiency? One naturally hesitates to add this note of discouragement to a book in which others of clearer vision will no doubt record the signs of returning balance and sanity among men.

Meanwhile, I have found, if not hope, at least moments of tragic purgation in another sort of reading. By chance I have been going through some of the plays of Euripides this summer, particularly those that deal with the disasters of Troy and Troy's besiegers, and the pathos of these scenes has blended strangely with the news that reaches me once a day from the city. Inevitably the imagination turns to comparisons between the present and the remote past. So, for instance, the very day that brought me the request to contribute to the Belgian relief I was reading the story

[133]

of Iphigenia, sacrificed in order that the Greek army might sail from
Aulis and reach its destination:

> O father! were the tongue of Orpheus mine,
> To charm the stones with song to follow me,
> And throw the spell of words on whom I would,
> So should I speak. But now, as I am wise
> In tears, and only tears, I speak through these.
> This body which my mother bore to thee,
> Low at thy knees I lay, imploring thus
> To spare my unripe youth. Sweet is the light
> To human eyes; oh! force me not to see
> Those dark things under earth! I first of all
> Called thee by name of "father"; heard "my child";
> I first here on thy knees gave and received
> The little, dear, caressing joys of love.
> And I recall thy words: "O girl," thou saidst,
> "Shall ever I behold thee in thy home
> Happy and prosperous as becomes thy sire?"
> And my words too, while then my tiny hand
> Clung to thy beard, as now I cling: "And I,
> Some day when thou art old, within my halls,
> Dearer for this, shall I receive thee, father;
> And with such love repay thy fostering care?"
> These words still in my memory lodge; but thou
> Must have forgotten, willing now my death.
> By Pelops and thy father Atreus, oh,
> And by my mother, who a second time
> Must travail for my life, oh, hear my prayer!
> Why should the wrongs of Helen fall on me,
> Or why came Paris for my evil fate?
> Yet turn thine eyes upon me, look and kiss,

That dying I at least may have of thee
This pledge of memory, if my prayer is vain.
O brother, little and of little aid,
Yet add thy tears to mine, and with them plead
To save thy sister. For in children still
Some sense of coming evil moves the heart.
See, father, how he pleads who cannot speak;
Thou wilt have mercy and regard my youth.

From this passage, which furnished Landor with the theme of one of the most beautiful, in some respects the most classical, of modern poems, it is natural to turn to the still more exquisite account of the death of Polyxena, the youngest daughter of Hecuba, slain as a peace-offering to the shade of Achilles. The brave words and self-surrender of the girl are related to the stricken mother by the herald Talthybius:

"O Argives, ye have brought my city low,
And I will die; yet, for I bare my throat,
Myself unflinching, touch me not at all.
As ye would please your gods, let me die free
Who have lived free; and slay me as ye will.
For I am queenly born, and would not go
As a slave goes to be among the dead."
Then all the people shouted, and the king
Called to the youths to set the maiden free;
And at the sheer command the young men heard,
And drew their hands away, and touched her not.
And she too heard the cry and the command;
Then straightway grasped her mantle at the knot,
And rent it downwards to the middle waist,
So standing like a statue, with her breast
And bosom bared, most beautiful, a moment;
Then kneeling spoke her last heroic words:

"This is my breast, O youth, if here the blow
  Must fall; or if thou choose my neck,
Strike; it is ready."
                       And Achilles' son,
Willing and willing not, for very ruth,
Cleft with his iron blade the slender throat,
And let the life out there. And this is true,
That even in death she kept her maiden shame,
And falling drew her robe against men's eyes.

These pathetic scenes, we should remember, were enacted before the people of Athens at a time when the lust of empire and the greed of expanding commerce had thrown Greece into a war which was to leave the land distracted and impoverished of its men, to be a prey to the ambitions of Alexander and the armies of Rome. What deep and poignant emotions Euripides stirred in the breasts of the spectators those can guess who have seen his *Iphigenia* and *Trojan Women* acted in English in these similar days of trial. And the *catharsis*, or tragic purgation, was the same then as now, only more perfect, no doubt, and purer. By these echoes of cruel deeds, ancient even in the years of the Peloponnesian war, the mind is turned from immediate calamities and apprehensions to reflecting on the fatality of sin and madness that rests on mankind, not now alone but at all times. With the tears shed for strange, far-off things, some part of the bitterness of our personal grief is carried away; the constriction of resentment, as if somehow Fate were our special enemy, is loosened, and the hatred of cruel men that clutches the heart is relaxed in pity for the everlasting tragedy of human life. Instead of rebellion we learn resignation. When at last Iphigenia surrenders herself to be a victim for the host, the chorus commend her act and draw this moral:

Noble and well, it is with thee, O child;
The will of fortune and the god is sick.

In later times Lucretius was to take up this thought, and in repeating the story of Iphigenia was to denounce the very notion of divine interference in perhaps the most terrible line that ever poet wrote:

Tantum religio potuit suadere malorum.

That is one way of regarding the evils of human destiny, as if they were the work of blind chance, but not the wise way; for at the end of such atheism only madness lies. The truer counsel is in that humility which faces the facts, yet acknowledges the impotence of man's reason to act as judge in these high matters. Christianity and paganism come close together in the lesson taught by Euripides:

O daughter, God is strange and all his ways
Past finding out. So for his own good will
He turns the fortunes of mankind about,
And hither thither moves.

That is the element of religious purgation which Euripides brought to the people of Athens when their whole horizon was darkened by war. But this is not all. Indeed, were this all, we should reject such consolation indignantly, as being akin to that form of humanitarianism which has been disintegrating modern society by throwing the responsibility for crime anywhere except on the individual delinquent. Euripides may have found alleviation in the universal mystery of evil, but neither he, in his better moments, nor any other of the true Greeks turned consolation into license, or doubted that a sure nemesis followed the infractions of justice, or the insolence of pride, or the errors of guilty ignorance:

Strong are the gods, and stronger yet the law
That sways them; even as by the law we know
The gods exist, and in our life divide
The bounds of right and wrong.

The madness of Troy and the Achaean army may have been the work of heaven, but no small part of Greek tragedy, from the *Agamemnon* of

Aeschylus to the *Hecuba* of Euripides, is taken up with the tale of retribution that came to this man and that for his arrogance or folly. So are consolation and admonition bound together. If their union in ancient ethics seems paradoxical, or even contradictory, it is nevertheless confirmed by the teaching of Christianity: For evil must come into the world, but woe unto him through whom it comes.

It is a curious and disquieting fact that the poet who was able to compress the moral of Greek tragedy into a single memorable stanza, belongs to the people who, if there is any truth in that moral, must shortly reckon with the nemesis appointed for sins of presumption and cruelty.

> Ihr zieht ins Leben uns hinein;
> Ihr lasst den armen schuldig werden;
> Dann überlasst ihr ihn der Pein;
> Denn alle Schuld rächt sich auf Erden.

PAUL ELMER MORE

JACQUES-ÉMILE BLANCHE

PORTRAIT OF GEORGE MOORE

FROM A PHOTOGRAPH OF THE ORIGINAL PAINTING

THE RUSSIAN BOGYMAN

THE devastating war in Europe has robbed the United States of one familiar figure, of one cherished illusion. In the stage setting of the nations, we have long expected Russia to play the villain's rôle. We have depended on her for dark deeds, we have owed to her our finest thrills of virtuous indignation. From the days when Mr. George Kennan worked the prolific Siberian prison vein (our own prison system was not then calculated to make us unduly proud), down to the summer of 1914, we have never failed to respond to any outcry against a nation about which we were reliably misinformed. It was quite the fashion, when I was young, for some thousands, or perhaps some millions of modest American citizens to sign a protest to the Czar, whenever we disapproved of the imperial policy. What became of these protests, nobody knew; the chance of the Czar's reading the millions of names seemed, even to us, unlikely; but it was our nearest approach to intimacy with the great and wicked ones of earth, and we felt we were doing our best to stem the tide of tyranny.

A great deal of this popular sentiment came to us from England, where hostility to Russia was bred of national fear. A great deal of it was fostered by Jewish immigrants in the United States. But the dislike of democracy for autocracy was responsible for our most cherished illusions.

Some god this severance rules.

A well-told story like Mr. Kipling's "The Man Who Was" seemed to us an indictment of a nation. Popular magazines cultivated a school of fiction in which Russian nobles were portrayed as living the unfettered lives, and enjoying the unfettered pastimes, of Dahomey chiefs. Popular melodrama showed us the heads of the Russian police department devoting themselves unreservedly to the persecution of innocent maidenhood. The only good Russian ever presented to us was the nihilist, some one who, like Mademoiselle Ixe, spent her time in pursuit of a nameless official, and shot him for a nameless crime. Even our admiration for Count Tolstoy was founded on his revolt from the established order of things in his own country. It seldom occurred to us that the established order of things in any other country would have been equally obnoxious to this thorough-paced reformer. New York would have been as little to his taste as was St. Petersburg.

The exigencies of a political alliance have impelled England to lay aside her former animosities, and bury them in oblivion. For many months she has tried hard to reinstate Russia in popular opinion, chiefly by means of serious papers in serious periodicals, which the populace never reads. Mr. Bernard Shaw is perhaps the only man left in the United Kingdom who clings desperately to the good old Russian bogyman, as we cling to the ogre of our infancy, and the pirate of our tender youth. Mr. Shaw's Russia is not merely a land where pure-minded, noble-hearted disturbers of the peace are subject to shameful captivity. It is a land where "people whose worst crime is to find the Daily News a congenial newspaper are hanged, flogged, or sent to Siberia, as a matter of daily routine." This is worse than Dahomey, where the perils of the press are happily unknown. Most of us would change our morning paper rather than be hanged. Few of us would find any journal "congenial," which paved the long way to Siberia.

England sympathized with Japan in the Japanese-Russian war from interested motives. We did the same out of pure unadulterated sentiment. Japan was an unfriendly power, given to hostile mutterings. Russia was a friendly power, which had done us more than one good turn. But Japan was little, and Russia was big. "How," asks the experienced Mr. Vincent Crummles, "are you to get up the sympathies of an audience in a legitimate manner, if there isn't a little man contending against a big one?" Japan, moreover, was the innocent land of cherry blossoms, and Russia was the land of knouts, and spies, and Cossacks. Russia worshipped God with rites and ceremonies, displeasing to pious Americans. Japan belonged to Heathendom, and merited enlightened tolerance.

A fresh deal in international policy may at any time sever and re-unite the troubled powers of Europe. Their boundary lines are hostages to fortune. But we, with two oceans sweeping our shores, have lost our bogyman beyond all hope of recovery. It is not with us a question of altered interests, but of altered values. Germany's campaign in Belgium has changed forever our standards of perfidy and of frightfulness. We can never go back to the old ones. Once we spoke of Russia as a nation

> Which to the good old maxim clings,
> That treaties are the pawns of Kings.

Now we know that Germany outstrips her far in faithlessness. Once we called Russia oppressive, cruel, unjust. Now the devastated homes of Flanders teach us the meaning of those words. Once we reproached Russia for being the least civilized of Christian nations. Now we have seen a potent civilization crash down into pure savagery, its flimsy restraints of no avail before the loosened passions of men.

And for our own share of injury and insult? Is it possible that a few years ago we deeply resented Russia's disrespect for American passports; that we abrogated a treaty because she dared to turn back from her frontiers American citizens armed with these sacred guarantees? To-day our dead lie under the ocean; and Germany, who sent them there, sings comic songs in her music halls to celebrate the rare jest of their drowning. Our sensitive pride which could brook no slight from the friendly hand of Russia, is now humbled to the dust by Germany's mailed fist. She has spared us no hurt, and she has spared us no jibe. Bleeding and bewildered, we have come to a realization of things as they are, we have seen the naked truth, and we can never go back to our illusions. We enjoyed our old bogyman, our shivers of horror, our exalted sentiments, our comfortable conviction of superiority. Now nothing is left but sorrow for our dead, and shame for the wrongs which have been done us. As long as history is taught, the tale of this terrible year will silence all other tales of horror. Not for us only, but for the listening world, the standard of uttermost evil has been forever changed.

Agnes Repplier

EDWIN HOWLAND BLASHFIELD

A WOMAN'S HEAD

FROM THE ORIGINAL DRAWING

Edwin Howland Blashfield
1915

CHANT DES GALLOISES

I

Voici que le soir tombe, avec l'orage. Et le soleil passionné descend, comme un blessé se traîne avec lenteur sur la colline: il descend sur la mer, avec un sourire, tout en sang. Et tout à l'heure, le divin Héros sera couché sur le lit qu'il préfère.

Voici que le soir tombe. Les jeunes filles de l'Ouest viennent sur la prairie; et viennent aussi les jeunes femmes de la douce terre. Elles sont deux chœurs qui se rencontrent dans l'herbe fleurie et l'odeur du blé noir, qui sont le miel et la vanille.

Elles s'avancent les unes vers les autres, les vierges et celles qui le furent, les nids à baisers et celles qui voudraient l'avoir été. Elles désireraient de danser: mais ni les amants, ni les fiancés ne sont plus là. Est-ce qu'ils sont tous morts? Ils sont tous partis pour l'œuvre dure et pour la guerre. Elles ne pourront plus fouler le raisin de la joie dans la danse. Et elles ne veulent pas danser aux bras l'une de l'autre. Il ne leur reste qu'à lancer leur âme dans le chant.

Chantez, les belles! L'heure du chant sonne pour vous, sur la prairie brûlante, entre le mur des chênes et les lèvres de l'océan. Allez, mes belles! Mettez-vous, les libres jeunes filles, au bord de la vague verte. Et vous, les jeunes femmes, contre la haie des feuilles au cœur déchiqueté, qui vous sépare de l'Orient.

II

LA JEUNE FILLE

Amour! un an de guerre! et les treize mois sont révolus! O fiancées que nous sommes! Douloureuses, pleines de sourires, avides de danser et tant déçues, où êtes-vous, nos fiancés?

Notre voix est toute chaude. Notre voix vient du feu, pour vous appeler. Beaux fiancés, où êtes-vous, si doux, si chers à celles qui vous attendent?

Nous ne danserons plus. Nous chanterons notre peine.

Une sœur, hier, a frappé dans la nuit, toc toc, sur nos portes, à la chambre des vierges.

Et vierge comme nous, elle est entrée tout en pleurs et nous a dit: " Je suis Poleska, la jeune fille de Pologne. Sœurs de Bretagne, sœurs galloises, savez-vous la danse et le chant, cet été, de vos sœurs polonaises? Elles sont la couronne et le tombeau. Elles vont, coquelicots de deuil et bleuets, par la plaine; et la bêche à la main, du matin au soir, elles creusent des fosses. Elles mettent dans la terre leurs fiancés et leurs amants. Voilà l'été de la Pologne, et nos couches nuptiales, ô sœurs de l'Occident."

Ayant dit son message, elle a pâli, la brune jeune fille de l'Orient, aux yeux si bleus, au visage si blanc; et baissant son col souple sur sa gorge, elle est morte en pleurant.

Et vous, qui êtes contre la haie, après ce long hiver dans la brume, ô tendres veuves du baiser, quel fut votre printemps? et quel est votre été? Vers nous levez les yeux, belles émeraudes mouillées. Répondez, blondes orphelines du soleil, chères sœurs galloises.

III

LA JEUNE FEMME

Nous sommes les amantes et les jeunes femmes. Petites sœurs, vous n'êtes que les fiancées.

Un an de dévorante amour et de regret! Une année dans le gouffre de l'ombre sèche! Un an de solitude et de douleur.

O petites sœurs, vous espérez la vie, même quand vous la pleurez. Mais nous, elle nous dévore.

Nous voici prêtes à mourir d'amour. Et vainement. Et nul ne veut notre don. Et notre cœur est inutile. Ah! C'est bien là le pis. Nous mourons de nous-mêmes et de tout.

Au plus tendre de nous, le désespoir ronge ce que le souvenir déchire. Fiancées, fiancées, vous ne savez pas les ardeurs des amantes, et que leurs larmes sont du sang.

.   .   .   .

Vous ne savez pas non plus, tu l'ignores encore, toi qui chantes, suave jeune fille, quelle moisson nous avons faite, et quel est ce cortège, là-bas, ouvrant la haie, qui s'avance sur la prairie, portant un trésor caché, comme une châsse dans les blés.

O ma sœur, toi qui es si chaude et la plus pâle, viens dans mes bras, si tu ne veux tomber.

Celui que ces jeunes femmes promènent sur leurs épaules, parmi les fleurs, c'est ton beau fiancé.

Il est mort d'amour pour Notre Dame, entre la mer et la Marne.

Il aimait.

IV

Comme le soleil rougit, d'une dernière effusion, toute la mer verte, on couche le beau jeune homme dans les seigles.

Il est mort. Il est nu, il est blanc dans les épis. Blanche est sa bouche, et ses yeux sont clos comme les portes du jour : silence éternel sur le rire, la lumière et le bruit.

Ses lèvres sont de cendres. La double flamme est morte. Plus de tison. Et la fleur virile est à jamais fauchée. Qu'il est beau, le jeune corps de l'homme ! Et le héros est toujours pur.

Elles le baisent toutes, cent fois, suavement, comme on mange le raisin à la grappe ; et les unes pleurent ; les autres sourient, telles de tendres folles.

C'est moi, l'amant ! C'est moi le fiancé, que vous portez ainsi, mes belles. C'est moi, le soc de la terre et le coutre d'amour que vous allez ensevelir dans l'herbe.

Et celle qui eût été mon champ, mourra sans fleurs et sans épis.

Du moins, sauvez-moi de la mort froide et de l'oubli.

Prenez moi dans votre paradis de femmes, entre vos lèvres.

Une heure encore, tenez moi et me serrez dans votre doux giron qui sent la menthe fraîche, le miel, le romarin et la brûlante giroflée.

Gardez moi, je vous prie, dans la chambre des baisers. Je me suis séparé de mes autres armes: immortelles, elles n'ont pas besoin de moi.

Et puisqu'il faut un linceul, cousez moi dans vos cheveux avec vos larmes. Cousez moi, à longues aiguillées de pleurs, dans vos ardents cheveux.

v

Si nous ne sommes amour, que sommes nous? Toutes, ici, nous voici vouées, adieu semailles! au soleil qui s'en va chaque soir et aux cruelles pluies.

Amants, nos bien aimés, tel est donc l'amour pour qui nous sommes nées? Mères, pourquoi fîtes-vous ces filles malheureuses? Nos âmes bondissent en révolte. Et tous nos cœurs qui veulent sortir de nous!

Baisons nous, sœurs chéries, au nom de l'amour et de la mort: et du Seigneur qui aime, qui ouvre au ciel les sources, et les parcs d'amour, pour tous les Aimés, au paradis.

— O belles, ô douloureuses, chantent les jeunes filles, vous qui êtes séparées de votre chair et de vos baisers, venez.

— Et vous, petites filles, disent les jeunes femmes, ô délicieuses, divisées de vos désirs, privées de votre attente et des caresses, venez.

— Chers cœurs!

— Chères femmes!

.   .   .   .

Elles pleurent, et se baisent doucement aux lèvres, avec un sourire.

Puis elles se sont saluées, en chantant, sous le portique de la nuit, tandis que l'océan dévorait les derniers tisons et les œillets suprêmes du couchant.

ANDRÉ SUARÈS

ANDRÉ SUARÈS

SONG OF THE WELSH WOMEN
[TRANSLATION]

HERE comes the night, with the storm. Slowly the passionate sun goes down; like a wounded man he drags himself over the hill; swimming in blood he sinks toward the sea. Soon the divine Hero will be laid on the bed of his choice.

Here comes the night. The maidens of the West come out across the meadows, and the young women of the land come out to meet them. Two singing choirs, they mingle in the flowered grass, and in the smell of the black wheat that is like the smell of honey and vanilla.

Forward they go to meet each other, maids and they that once were maids—nests of kisses, and those that willingly would be so. They long to dance, but lovers and bridegrooms are far away: all have gone out to the stern work of war. No more can the women tread the red wine of joy in the dance; they have no mind to dance with one another, and so they sing instead.

Begin, fair women! The hour of your song has come, in the hot meadows between the dark wall of oaks and the pale lips of ocean. Come! Take your places, you free-limbed maidens, by the green wave, and you, young women, by the hedge-rows with fretted leaves that stand between you and the east.

II
THE YOUNG GIRL SPEAKS

Love!—and a year of war! The twelvemonth has fulfilled itself, and one month more! Sorrowful and full of smiles, eager to dance and pale with waiting—tell us, our lovers, where you linger!

Our voices are warm, our voices come from the fire to call you. Where are you, our lovers, you that are so dear to those who wait?

[147]

We have forsworn the dance, and grief shall be the burden of our song.

Yesterday, in the night, a sister came knock-knocking at our door, the door of the virgins. A maid as we are maids, she came in to us, all weeping, and said:

"I am the daughter of Poland. Sisters of Britain, sisters of Wales, do you know the dance that your Polish sisters dance, and the songs they sing? The grave and the funeral garland are their song. Like black poppies and dark corn-flowers sprinkled on the plain, they move in sad lines, from night to morning digging graves; and in those graves they lay their bridegrooms and their lovers. This, my sisters, has the summer brought to Poland, and these have been our bridal beds."

And having spoken, the daughter of the East grew pale, and drooped her dark head upon her neck and died.

And you who stand beside the hedge-rows, what was your spring-time, what your heavy summer? Turn toward us the wet emeralds of your eyes : answer, golden daughters of the sun—our sisters of Wales !

III

THE YOUNG WOMAN SPEAKS

We are the young women and the beloved. Little sisters, what are you but the betrothed?

A year of devouring love, a year of longing; long year in the valley of parched shadow—year of loneliness and grief!

See, we are dying of love, and none to slake us. Worst waste of all, our hearts are useless; we are dying of ourselves and of all life. O young girls, little do you know of the hearts of women beloved, and lovers' tears like blood!

Little do you know of the harvest we have reaped, or of the meaning of that funeral train that comes across the meadows, parting the hedges to right and left and bearing a hidden treasure like a monstrance born across the wheat.

O my sister, burning hot and palest, come to me lest you fall, and let me hold you.

He whom the young women carry on their shoulders, knee-deep in flowers, was your once lover.

Between the sea and the Marne he died for love of our Lady, the Blessed Virgin. He loved . . .

IV

As the last flush of sunset suffuses the green ocean the young man is laid amid the wheat.

He is dead. White and naked he lies among the wheat-ears. White are his lips, and his eyes are closed like the eyes of the day. His laughter, the light and sound of him, are gone.

His mouth is ashes. The double flame of his lips is dead. In its flower his manhood is cut down. How beautiful is the young man's body! And stainless is the body of the hero.

The women bend to kiss him one by one, slowly, lingeringly, as grapes are eaten from the vine; and some weep, and others laugh, beside themselves for grieving.

I am the lover, whom you thus bear upon your shoulders; young maidens, I am the betrothed. I am the ploughshare in the wheatfield, whom thus you lay down for burial. And she who should have been my field and my harvest shall die without flower and without ripening.

Save me at least, O pitying women, from the cold earth and from oblivion. Keep me warm in the paradise of your lips, an hour longer keep me among you, in the sweet air that smells of honey and rosemary, of clove-pinks and the flowering mint.

Build about me the warm chamber of your kisses. My sword and my shield are gone from me; deathless, they have no need of the dead.

And for my shrouding, women, wind me about with your long hair, and sew my shroud with your tears. With the long needles of your tears sew me fast into your burning hair.

V

If we are not Love and the food of Love, what are we? Our blossoming cut down, we follow the setting sun into darkness and the night of rain.

Lovers, our beloved, is this the love for which our mothers bore us? O mothers, why bring us forth to such grieving? Our souls leap up against our fate, and our hearts break from our bosoms.

Kiss us, young sisters, in the name of Love and Death; and of the Lord of Love, who is King of its fountains and gardens, and opens their gates to the Beloved in Paradise.

O fair and stricken and undone—the young maids answer—come to us, you who are parted from the lips that cherished you and the flesh of your flesh.

And you, young maidens—the mourning women reply to them—you, who have missed your dream and your fruition, come to us, dear hearts.

Poor wives . . . Poor maids!

They weep, and kiss each other, and clasp each other smiling through their sorrow.

Then, singing, they part beneath the roof of night, while Ocean consumes the last embers of day, and darkens under the sky incarnadine.

ANDRÉ SUARÈS

ÉMILE-RENÉ MÉNARD

FIGURE

WORDSWORTH'S VALLEY IN WAR–TIME

Aᴜɢᴜsᴛ 8ᵗʰ, 1915. It is now four days since, in this village of Grasmere, at my feet, we attended one of those anniversary meetings, marking the first completed year of this appalling war, which were being
called on that night over the length and breadth of England. Our meeting was held in the village schoolroom; the farmers, tradesmen, inn-
keeper and summer visitors of Grasmere were present, and we passed
the resolution which all England was passing at the same moment,
pledging ourselves, separately and collectively, to help the war and continue the war, till the purposes of England were attained, by the liberation of Belgium and northern France, and the chastisement of Germany.

A year and four days, then, since the war began, and in a remote
garden on the banks of the Forth, my husband and I passed, breathless,
to each other, the sheets of the evening paper brought from Edinburgh
by the last train, containing the greater part of Sir Edward Grey's speech
delivered in the House of Commons that afternoon — War for Belgium —
for national honour — and, in the long run, for national existence! War!
—after these long years of peace; war, with its dimly foreseen horrors,
and its unfathomed possibilities:—England paused and shivered as the
grim spectre stepped across her path.

And I stand to-night on this lovely mountain-side, looking out upon
the harvest fields of another August, and soon another evening newspaper sent up from the village below will bring the latest list of our dead
and our maimed, for which English mothers and wives have looked in
terror, day after day, through this twelve months.

And yet, but for the brooding care in every English mind, how could
one dream of war in this peaceful Grasmere?

Is it really true that somewhere in this summer world, beyond those
furthest fells, and the Yorkshire moors behind them, beyond the silver
sea dashing its waves upon our Eastern coasts, there is still going on the

ruin, the agony, the fury, of this hideous struggle into which Germany plunged the world, a year ago? It is past eight o'clock; but the sun which is just dipping behind Silver How is still full on Loughrigg, the beautiful fell which closes in the southern end of the lake. Between me and these illumined slopes lies the lake—shadowed and still, broken by its one green island. I can just see the white cups of the water-lilies floating above the mirrored woods and rocks that plunge so deep into the infinity below.

The square tower of the church rises to my left. The ashes of Wordsworth lie just beyond it—of Wordsworth, and that sister with the "wild eyes," who is scarcely less sure of immortality than himself, of Mary Wordsworth too, the "perfect woman, nobly planned," at whose feet, in her white-haired old age, I myself as a small child of five can remember sitting, nearly sixty years ago. A little further, trees and buildings hide what was once the grassy margin of the lake, and the old coach road from Ambleside, with Wordsworth's cottage upon it. Dove Cottage, where "mighty poets" gathered, and poetry that England will never let die was written, is now, as all the world knows, a national possession, and is full of memorials not only of Wordsworth, his sister and his wife, but of all the other famous men who haunted there—De Quincey, who lived there for more than twenty years, Southey and Coleridge; or of Wordsworth's younger contemporaries and neighbours in the Lakes, such as Arnold of Rugby, and Arnold's poet son Matthew. Generally the tiny house and garden are thronged by Americans in August, who crowd—in the Homeric phrase—about the charming place, like flies about the milk pails in summer.

But this year there are no Americans, there are few visitors, indeed, of any kind as yet, though the coaches are beginning to bring them—scantily. But Grasmere does not distress itself as it would in other years, Wordsworth's village is thinking too much about the war. Before the war —so I learn from a gentle lady, who is one of the most eager guardians of Grasmere traditions, and has made remarkable and successful efforts, through the annual "Grasmere play," which is her creation, to maintain the rich old dialect of the dales—there were *two* Grasmere men in the Navy, *two* soldiers in the Regular army, and *three* Reservists—out of a total male population of all ages of three hundred and eighty-nine. No one ever saw a soldier, and wages, as all over the north, were high. There was some perplexity of mind among the dale-folk when war broke out. France and Belgium seemed a long way off—more than "t'oother side o' Kendal," a common measure of distance in the mind of the old folks, whose schooling lies far behind them; and fighting seemed a strange thing to these men of peace. "What!—there'll be nea fightin'!" said an old man in the village, the day before war was declared. "There's nea blacks amongst 'em [meaning the Germans]—they'se civilised beings!" But the fighting came, and Grasmere did as Grasmere did in 1803, when Pitt called for volunteers for Home Defence. "At Grasmere," wrote Wordsworth, "we have turned out almost to a man." Last year, within a few months of the outbreak of war, seventy young men from the village offered themselves to the army; over fifty are serving. Their women left behind have been steadily knitting and sewing since they left. Every man from Grasmere got a Christmas present of two pairs of socks. Two sisters, washerwomen, and hard worked, made a pair each, in four consecutive weeks, getting up at four in the morning to knit. Day after day, women from the village have gone up to the fells to gather the absorbent sphagnum moss, which they dry and clean, and send to a manufacturing chemist to be prepared for hospital use. Half a ton of feather-weight moss has been collected and cleaned by women and school-children. One old woman who could not give money gathered the tufts of wool which the sheep leave behind them on the brambles and fern, washed them, and made them into the little pillows which prop wounded limbs in hospital. The cottages and farms send eggs every week to the wounded in France. The school-children alone bring fifty a week. One woman, whose main resource was her fowls, offered twelve eggs a week; which meant starving herself. And all the time, two pence, three pence, six pence a week was being collected by the people themselves, from the poorest homes, towards the support of the Belgian colony in the neighbouring village of Ambleside.

One sits and ponders these things, as the golden light recedes from Loughrigg, and that high crag above Wordsworth's cottage. Little Grasmere has indeed done all she could, and in this lovely valley, the heart of Wordsworth's people, the descendants of those dalesmen and daleswomen whom he brought into literature, is one—passionately one—with the heart of the Allies. Lately the war has bitten harder into the life of the village. Of its fifty young sons, many are now in the thick of the Dardanelles struggle; three are prisoners of war, two are said to have gone down in the Royal Edward, one officer has fallen, others are wounded. Grasmere has learnt much geography and history this last year; and it has shared to the full in the general deepening and uplifting of the English soul, which the war has brought about. France, that France which Wordsworth loved in his first generous youth, is in all our hearts,— France, and the sufferings of France; Belgium, too, the trampled and outraged victim of a Germany eternally dishonoured. And where shall we find nobler words in which to clothe the feeling of England towards a France which has lost Rheims, or a Belgium which has endured Louvain, than those written a hundred years ago in that cottage across the lake?

> Air, earth and skies—
> There's not a breathing of the common wind
> That will forget thee; thou hast great allies;
> Thy friends are exultations, agonies,
> And love, and man's unconquerable mind!

To Germany, then, the initial weight of big battalions, the initial successes of a murderous science : to the nations leagued against her, the unconquerable power of those moral faiths which fire our clay, and in the end mould the history of men!

. . . Along the mountain-side, the evening wind rises. The swell and beat of it among the rocks and fern, as the crags catch it, echo it, and throw it back reverberate, are as the sound of marching feet. . . .

I hear it in the tread—irresistible, inexorable—of an avenging Humanity. The living and the dead are there, and in their hands they bear both Doom and Comforting.

MARY A. WARD

THE BOOK OF THE HOMELESS

Printed and Bound in China by C & C Offset Joint Printing Co.

Printed on 157 gsm Chinese matte art paper
Bound in Fai Mei cloth

DISTRIBUTED BY DOVER PUBLICATIONS, INC.